more
not so big
solutions
for your home

more
not so big
solutions
for your home

Sarah Susanka

The Taunton Press

The Taunton Press
Inspiration for hands-on living®

The Taunton Press, Inc.
63 South Main Street, PO Box 5506
Newtown, CT 06470-5506
e-mail: tp@taunton.com

Editors: Carolyn Mandarano, Marie St. Hilaire
Copy editor: Diane Sinitsky
Jacket/Cover design: Jean-Marc Troadec
Interior design: Mary McKeon
Layout: Cathy Cassidy
Illustrator: Sarah Susanka and Scott Bricher

Library of Congress Cataloging-in-Publication Data

Susanka, Sarah.
  More not so big solutions for your home / author, Sarah Susanka.
    p. cm.
  ISBN 978-1-60085-148-3
  1. Architecture, Domestic. 2. Interior architecture. 3. Small houses. 4. Architecture--Composition, proportion, etc. I. Title.
  NA7115.S873 2010
  728'.37--dc22

                          2009044904

Printed in the United States of America
10 9 8 7 6 5 4 3 2

The following names/manufacturers appearing in *More Not So Big Solutions for Your Home* are trademarks:
Corian®, IKEA®, Pottery Barn®, West Elm®

Acknowledgments

There are three separate groups of people I want to thank for helping to bring this book into being, and their involvement stretches over a decade.

First, there are the good folks at *Fine Homebuilding*, who made it possible for me to bring these ideas to market in each issue of their fabulous magazine from 1999 through 2004. The articles from that magazine that appear here are from 2002 onward, when my editors were Dan Morrison, Sean Groom, and Charles Miller. Kevin Ireton, who was the editor for the magazine until early 2009 and who first invited me to begin writing for *Fine Homebuilding*, was also a big part of making these articles such a success. To this day I still hear from devoted *Fine Homebuilding* subscribers who tell me they loved my columns and are so glad they're now available in book form.

At the end of 2004, I jumped ship to contribute to *Inspired House* magazine, another Taunton publication, where I contributed a column each issue until the magazine closed its doors in 2006. So the second thank-you goes to the editors there. While writing for *Inspired House*, Anne Corey helped pare down my often too wordy articles to the appropriate length. (I may be an expert on Not So Big houses, but I'm not very good at not so long articles!) Those who are familiar with the magazine may notice that the chapters in this book are longer than the originally published articles. That's because we were able to include some of the material that had to be left out in the necessarily shorter form of the magazine version. Anne, Jan Senn (the editor of *Inspired House*), and everyone who worked on the publication deserve enormous credit for assembling a wonderful, though sadly short-lived magazine. Someday another version of this same kind of magazine, targeted at homeowners who want to learn not only about interior design but about residential architecture as well, will arise again, and I hope to be a part of it.

And finally, there are my current editors, Carolyn Mandarano at The Taunton Press and Marie St. Hilaire here at Susanka Studios, who formed a terrific and efficient team approach to accomplish the task of assembling and shaping the articles into book form, with some expert supervision and organizational advice from behind the scenes by Peter Chapman.

Thanks to you all. I couldn't have done any of this without you.

Contents

Introduction

Little did I know when I began writing down what I had come to learn as a residential architect that I would be starting a Not So Big movement. But that's what it has turned into over the past decade, with an ever increasing audience of enthusiastic participants. As our economic fortunes turned in 2008, exactly one decade after *The Not So Big House* was first published, it became clear that the principles of Not So Big living provided a road map to a better and more sustainable way of building homes for the way we actually live.

When I first began talking about smaller, better-designed homes, I often attracted quizzical looks from people wanting to know why anyone would want to downsize—or right-size, as I prefer to call it. But Not So Big fans knew. They weren't interested in houses that were all square footage and volume but no soul. They wanted homes that were comfortable to live in, highly functional, and designed for their particular way of living. They understood that impressing the neighbors with size and volume has nothing to do with their dreams of home. They wanted to live in a place that really reflected who they were as people, that gave them a secure and beautiful sanctuary from which to launch themselves into the busy world each day, and that gave them a comfortable place to return for some much-needed respite when all their external obligations were completed. They knew instinctively that the quality of home is far more important than the quantity.

For many years, starting shortly after that first book came out, I began writing a regular column for Taunton Press's popular magazine *Fine Homebuilding*. These articles were lapped up by readers eager to learn more about how to tailor a home to fit its owners to a tee. After five years I decided, with the help of the folks at Taunton, to publish a volume of these articles, called *Not So Big Solutions for Your Home*. Unlike my other books, because of the original articles' format, the chapters in this book allowed me to go into the common problems faced by homeowners in a more detailed and information-packed way. The resulting book was very positively received, and it was clear that, once enough articles had been assembled for another volume, it would be a natural extension of the first. That's what you have in your hands now—*More Not So Big Solutions for Your Home*—the compilation of all the other articles about house design that I've written for Taunton Press magazines since early 2002.

But it's not just the rest of the *Fine Homebuilding* series you'll find here. This book also includes the 15 articles I wrote for another Taunton magazine, *Inspired House*.

That publication, which was written primarily for homeowners rather than for builders and designers as *Fine Homebuilding* is, had a deeply loyal fan base, many of whom, when the magazine folded in 2006, wrote to tell the editors (and me) how sad they were that it was gone.

I'm told that the "Not So Big Solutions" column was the favorite article issue after issue, proving what I've always known—that homeowners want to know more about their homes than just how to make them look good on the surface. They want to understand what gives a house good bones and how to improve those bones to maximize their home's potential for both comfort and practicality.

And that's what this book offers—a wealth of information and advice on how to make your home all it can be by learning to see beyond the surface problems and challenges to the potential that lies in wait of exploration. There's a huge wealth of commonsense and creative problem solving collected here that I hope will give you the tools you need to bring out the best in your home.

You can visit me at www.notsobighouse. com, where there are many more resources to help you, including hundreds of links to information about everything from sustainability to new urbanism, as well as a Home Professionals Directory for locating architects,

designers, builders, and remodelers who understand what Not So Big is all about. Whatever your home's challenges and no matter the size and scope, I wish you every success, and I hope you'll let me know how it goes.

ONE

By Design

When an architect begins to think about a new project, whether it's a remodeling, an addition, or a new home, there are a few design considerations he or she must address before doing anything else. These broad-based considerations—from how to allow for natural light to what kind of living space you need—are often overlooked by people not trained in architectural design, and yet they are important because they provide a point of orientation for the rest of the home's design.

For example, let's say you are planning to build a new home on a relatively small lot in an inner-ring suburb. The neighboring houses are mostly two stories and built between the 1920s and 1940s; there are no alleys in the area, so driveways typically run along one side of each lot to access a detached garage at the back. This setup gives the neighborhood a distinct flavor, and integrating the new home seamlessly into its environment requires thoughtful design. The new home will have some different features than its older neighbors, but it must still be designed to look like one of the pack if it is to fit in.

Perhaps you really want an attached garage. While there are no rules to prohibit a garage on the front of the house, facing the street, to place the garage there would be an anomaly and most likely an affront to the neighbors. So the architect's job is to figure out a way to include the attached garage the homeowners want but tuck it away on the back of the house and provide access from a driveway that looks very much like the other driveways on the street.

This type of thoughtful attention to the characteristics of the existing neighborhood is one example of the kind of design thinking that gives an architect the ground rules for proceeding with the plans for the home. The five broad-brush issues we'll look at here will give you a sense of how to orient yourself to your own design challenges and teach you how to think like an architect as he or she begins the work. Although the challenges presented here aren't the only ones to consider when beginning a new design project, they will help you to make the most of your budget while tailoring your home to fit your household, your activities, and your aesthetic and functional requirements to a tee.

Designing for Our Human Scale

It's obvious that houses are built for people, but what's not always so apparent is that good residential architecture is designed for our human scale. What exactly does that mean, though? Human beings come in a variety of shapes and sizes, so in home design a "one size fits all" approach won't work. But sadly, in residential construction today, with our love of bigness, houses have become vast in almost every direction. While these houses are impressive in a photograph, they are difficult to settle into because they're simply too large. It may be desirable to design a public building so that its visitors feel insignificant and awed by its scale, but that's hardly what we want for our own homes.

Before you start building or adding on, it's important to understand how to design spaces that will allow most people to feel comfortable. There are some standards and conventions with respect to the heights of things inside the house that can help us to tailor interior spaces to fit our bodies. The heights of windows and countertops are perfect examples.

Human beings come in all shapes and sizes, so in home design a "one size fits all" approach won't work.

Door and window heights

It is conventional to make the head of a standard doorway 6 ft. 8 in. above the floor. The tops of windows are also typically located at this height. In fact, I like to make both doors and windows exactly the same height off the floor so that all the heads (the tops) align perfectly. This looks more orderly and allows you to run a continuous trim band above them if you want to, tying them all together.

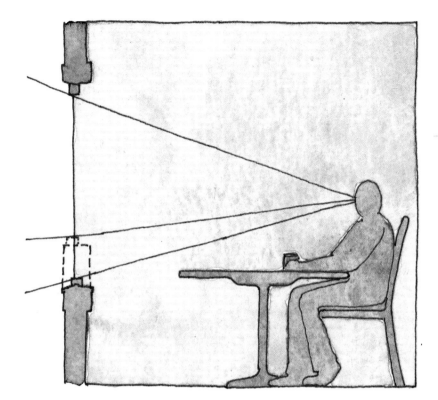

Lower sill heights to improve views. Locate windowsills about 2 ft. 4 in. off the floor to get the best view out and down to the surrounding landscape.

There aren't any conventions about windowsill heights though. Often they are located too high to see out of comfortably when you are sitting down. There are thousands of eat-in kitchens and breakfast nooks around the country that would be lovely spaces but for the height of the windowsill, which puts the sitter just out of eyeshot of the backyard or the view beyond.

To fix the problem, the key is to locate the sill sufficiently lower than your eye height so that when you are sitting on the far side of the table, you can still look out and down. My favorite sill height is about 2 ft. 4 in. from the floor to the bottom of the glass. When the sill is 3 ft. off the floor, you're definitely limiting access to exterior views.

The same sill height is desirable in a bedroom or a bathroom where you want to be able to see a view from the bed or the tub. Of course, this is recommended only for places where there's plenty of privacy from neighbors, or where you have window coverings that can obscure the lower part of the window if necessary.

Higher windowsill heights are needed where privacy is important—for instance, in most bathrooms—or where view does not matter and the window is simply there to let light in—maybe above a bed. In these situations,

Design windows for privacy. In rooms where you want privacy, like bathrooms and bedrooms, windows are best placed above chest height.

the best sill height is just above chest level, so you can still see out when you are next to the window without revealing any body parts that you don't want to show off to the neighbors.

At kitchen countertops, I like to bring the windows down as close as I can to countertop height so that the view is maximized. A 4-in. backsplash behind a standard countertop makes the windowsill height about 3 ft. 4 in. off the floor. You can also take the sill all the way down to the countertop height, which is usually 3 ft. off the floor.

Countertop and cabinet heights

In kitchens, most appliances are made to fit beneath a countertop that's 3 ft. off the floor. Therefore, this is the typical kitchen work surface height. Although it's not ideal for someone taller or shorter than average, it seems to satisfy most people most of the time. I've had many clients request either a taller or a shorter countertop, but I usually encourage them to stay with the standard 3-ft. height for the primary work areas. What's right for one homeowner may not be right for the next buyer of the home, and the need to replace all lower cabinetry in a kitchen can drive potential home buyers away.

Adding a lowered or raised section to an island or peninsula is a good alternative. A baking-center countertop that's 3 in. to 4 in. lower than usual makes kneading dough and rolling out pastry easier. And a small section of raised countertop can work well even for a short person, for setting out ingredients and items that are not currently in use. For the taller person, this will be the preferred food preparation area. All this may seem an exaggerated concern for anyone in the middle of the height spectrum, but for those taller or shorter than average it can make an enormous difference in convenience and comfort.

Vary counter heights according to use. Countertop heights can be changed to accommodate people of different heights and their kitchen activities, like kneading dough or chopping veggies.

Upper cabinets pose another challenge. I've heard from many shorter clients that upper cabinets are not very useful because they are simply too high. For this reason, I'll typically locate the upper cabinets 15 in. above the countertop, even though the convention today is often higher. Because the upper cabinets are shallower than the lower ones, and therefore don't obstruct the work surface below, the 15-in. height makes more of the cabinet area accessible to most people.

Ceiling heights

Because 2x4s, the most common building materials for residential construction, come in standard lengths of 8 ft., 9 ft., and 10 ft., most ceilings are one of these heights. In our love of spaciousness, ceiling heights

Adding a lowered or raised section to an island or peninsula is a good alternative to the typical kitchen work surface height.

have risen rapidly over the past two decades, and many houses today are built with 10-ft. studs. Although there is nothing inherently wrong with ceilings of this height, if the entire house is this tall, you can end up feeling somewhat diminutive yourself and often less comfortable. So I recommend always varying the ceiling heights—having places that are shorter, from 7 ft. to 8 ft. tall—as a contrast to the taller ones.

My preference is the standard 8-ft. ceiling, with some select lower-ceilinged areas, because it is closer to the heights of our human bodies and so is human scaled. Since it's also generally a little less expensive to build with 8-ft. studs than 9-ft. or 10-ft. studs, I prefer to save the money on height and add some special features with the money that's saved.

In recent years, 8-ft. ceilings have gotten a bad rap and are often thought of as boring, but they are only boring when the ceilings are the same height throughout the house. An all 9-ft. or all 10-ft. ceiling is just as bad. It's the variety that makes the house feel comfortable as well as interesting.

If you are planning a vaulted or cathedral ceiling, make sure the height of the peak doesn't overpower the size of the room. If you lower the spring line—the height of the vertical sidewall—the overall proportions of the room can feel significantly more appropriately scaled for our bodies. If you've ever visited a Cape Cod style house, you'll know what I mean. With a spring line of from 4 ft. 6 in. to 6 ft., the rooms on the upper level of such a home feel comfortable; the same-sized room with a higher spring line starts to feel more "cathedral" like, literally, which isn't a comfortable proportioning for a sleeping room.

Start taking note of the heights of things that you feel comfortable with. It's only by noticing how you feel in relationship to the heights of surfaces around you that you can replicate that scale in your own home. Your own body is your best gauge of what feels appropriately scaled to you.

8-ft. ceilings have gotten a bad rap and are often thought of as boring, but they are only boring when the ceilings are the same height throughout the house.

How Much Space Do You Really Need?

After having written the series of Not So Big House books, I get a lot of questions from people who want to know how much house is enough. They want rules and standards by which to gauge the right amount. But you can't define space this way for two reasons. First, a house that has a sense of home has almost nothing to do with square footage; and second, Not So Big means building a house about a third smaller than you thought you needed with dollars reapportioned out of square footage and into quality and character. Both of these points are intended to take the focus off quantity and place it firmly on the things that affect livability.

So where do you start, and how do you know whether the amount of space you are living in or plan to live in is not too big, too small, or just right? The following rules of thumb will help you determine whether it's more quantity of space you need or more quality you're really seeking. Although the answer is usually a combination of the two, our typical solution these days is to favor more quantity over more quality, when almost always it's an increase in quality of living environment that really makes us feel more comfortable and more at home.

The challenges related to figuring out how much space you will need in a new home are significantly greater than determining space needs when remodeling. The reason for this is that the homeowners of the house to be remodeled can pinpoint right away what works and what doesn't in their existing home. Although they may not be able to devise the perfect solution, they can see the problems they're facing with great clarity. Their challenge is to avoid jumping to the most obvious and simplest solution to their problems, which is almost always too big and which frequently spoils the character and utility of the existing space.

Adding space but not much square footage

1. An awkward rear entry delivers people directly into the kitchen.

2. The half-bath has only a toilet and a sink, so there's no reason for it to be as large as it is.

3. The circa-1975 kitchen is where most of the family living occurs.

4. The dining room is isolated, making it difficult to use. The heirloom table isn't appropriate for family use.

5. The large entry hall is wasted space because the family always uses the back door.

6. The living room is rarely used because it is too formal for everyday purposes.

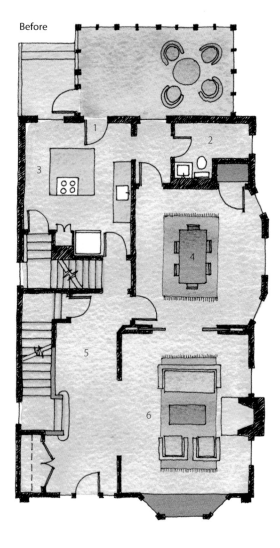

Before

What to Consider when Remodeling

1. Identify the problem areas and rooms.

2. Take an inventory of the rooms you already have, including dimensions and frequency of use.

3. Look for spaces that can be connected to meet your needs.

4. Look for spaces that can do double duty.

5. Only after these steps, consider adding on.

6. Determine what the existing roof form will let you do.

7. Make sure the scale of any added space matches that of the existing house.

To orient and ground the discussions, let's take two households as examples, one of which plans to remodel and one that plans to build from scratch.

Remodeling to incorporate Not So Big

John and Cindy live in a fine old Victorian with their three young children. The house is beautiful, but most of the space on the main floor is poorly suited to their needs. They spent most of their time while at home either cooped up in the inhospitable kitchen or sitting around the formal dining room table, inherited from Cindy's mom, worrying all the while about whether the children would damage it.

They wanted a new kitchen, an informal eating area, a place for their kids to play or watch TV while Cindy is in the kitchen, and an in-home office on the main level. Since

John and Cindy are both tall, they love the 10-ft. ceilings throughout the house. And they want whatever additions they make to match the character of the rest of the house. The remodeled floor plan involves very little additional square footage, but it does give the family lots more room (illustrations above and facing page).

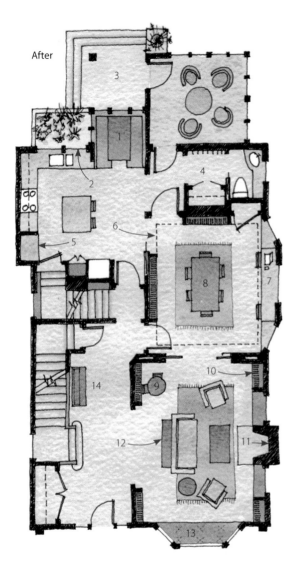

After

1. A new informal eating area with a great view of the backyard was added to the kitchen.

2. Bigger kitchen windows provide a better connection to the backyard.

3. The size of the screened porch was reduced and a new back entry created.

4. The half-bath was reduced in size to make room for a mudroom.

5. A 2-ft. bumpout provides room for a counter without having to move the basement stairs, which would have been expensive. There is no window on this side because of the proximity of the neighbors.

6. A section of the wall was removed to create a connection between the kitchen and the dining room.

7. A computer desk was added to the dining room, making it a multipurpose room. Bookshelves are on the opposite wall.

8. The heirloom table has a new protective covering, so it can be used for homework and bill paying, as well as for dining.

9. A small table and chairs in the living room provide a spot for card games and jigsaw puzzles.

10. Bookshelves on four walls make the room feel more comfortable and less formal.

11. A flat-screen TV above the fireplace is a new attraction to the living room.

12. The furniture is rearranged to make it more user friendly.

13. An upholstered cushion on the window seat creates a comfortable, cozy nook.

14. Since mail is delivered at the front of the house, this is a perfect place for a mail-sorting center.

Building a new Not So Big house

For a couple thinking about a new home, the plans they look at on paper typically don't give them enough information to gauge what the space will feel like when construction is complete. Reading plans is one thing, but lots of people have a hard time visualizing, for example, how big a 14-ft. by 16-ft. room will feel.

Because there's an almost universal fear of feeling too cramped—what I have termed "fear of too smallness"—would-be homeowners tend to make everything a bit bigger than their favored plan suggests, just to be on the safe side. This is one of the primary reasons

What to Consider when Building New

1. Measure and inventory the rooms you live in now and identify dimensions and frequency of use.

2. As you look at building plans, or as you work with an architect, keep the proportions of your existing home in mind.

3. Don't build spaces you use less than a handful of times a year.

4. Identify rooms that can do double duty.

5. Select a design whose proportions match those of your favorite houses.

6. Always get measurements of the spaces you plan to build, including the ceiling height of each, before committing to a design.

7. If you think something might be too big, try to find a model home with similar proportions to visit, to see how the space makes you feel.

8. Find someone you can trust to help you with the design, and then listen to his or her advice.

1. The back of the house is the main entry for family members, and it's ugly, cramped, and unwelcoming.

2. The front entry is dark and cramped.

3. The kitchen is small and awkward, with limited counter space and no informal eating area.

4. The pantry is one feature that works.

5. The formal dining room is completely separate from the kitchen. Most meals are eaten in the den.

6. The den, where most of the living in the house happens, is too far from the kitchen for easy communication during food prep.

7. The formal living room is rarely used. It's the biggest room but is not easily visible from the lived-in areas of the house.

The Old House

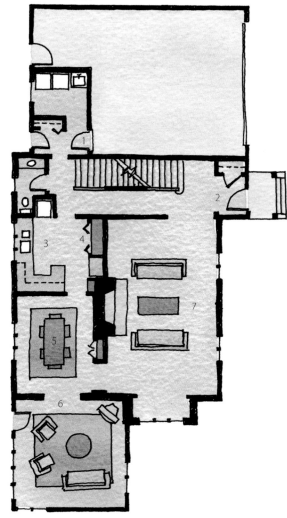

our culture's new houses have tended to keep escalating in size, with the result that a lot of households find themselves at sea in an ocean of space that is never too small but also never too comfortable.

In this example of building new, the Winston family wanted a house with more character. They also wanted a layout that would make family interaction easier during

food prep but that would still allow them to do different activities, such as homework or reading, within a shared living space so they could still be together as a family.

Doug and Julie Winston and their 13-year-old daughter, Laura, lived in their existing house for a dozen years before deciding to build a new house. Although there was enough space in it for three, the kitchen

The New House

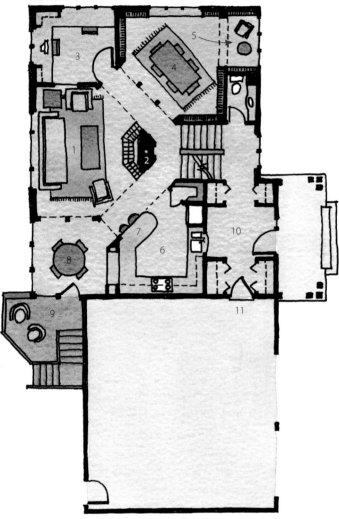

1. The one living area is comfortable and appropriate for both everyday living and formal occasions.

2. A flat-screen TV is mounted above the fireplace.

3. The office/away room can be separated acoustically by closing the door, but it remains connected visually to the living area with an interior window.

4. The formal dining room does double duty as library and homework area.

5. A library alcove offers a quiet, cozy place to read.

6. The kitchen has plenty of counter space, a walk-in pantry, and connection to surrounding spaces.

7. The breakfast bar offers a place to socialize during meal preparation.

8. The informal eating area has a lovely view and a strong connection to the kitchen.

9. The small back deck connects to the garden.

10. The pleasant and light-filled front entry can be seen from the kitchen overlook half a level above.

11. The family entry also opens to the welcoming front foyer.

Dotted lines indicate ceiling-height change.

offered little counter space and no place to eat without retiring to the dining room. They like to entertain, so they wanted a dining room that could be used to serve two to four guests. And the living room, while large, was not used much because it's not in the primary circulation path through the house. Instead, the den, which opens off the dining room, became their primary living space. They liked it because its size is comfortable for the three of them to gather and socialize.

The new house, illustration above, solves the problems in their previous house and gets rid of unused rooms. The multiuse spaces are welcoming and appropriately sized; changes in ceiling height help to define boundaries in the mostly open floor plan.

What Is an Open Plan and Why Does It Work?

We often forget to consider the ceiling as an element that defines our living spaces.

Open plan is a term coined by Frank Lloyd Wright to describe his revolutionary approach to home design. For centuries, houses were made up of boxes (rooms) connected by doorways and hallways. Wright spoke of the "destruction of the box"—eliminating walls on the inside to create spaces that flowed inside and outside to become one continuous, organic space. He suggested that instead of each function in the house being enclosed in its own separate box, rooms could be opened wide to one another. Light would filter from one area to another, circulation between areas would improve, and spaces would no longer be defined by one term, like "living room" or "dining room." Spaces would be differentiated from each other with changes in ceiling height, as well as with framed openings and columns, rather than with walls alone.

The kitchen becomes acceptable

You can see the beginnings of Wright's new vision for a house in his early work. Often a living room, dining room, and entry hall all opened gracefully into one another, so that from each space it was possible to see what was going on in the others (illustration facing page). Even more revolutionary

Open-plan origins.
Early designs by Frank Lloyd Wright had an openness that was influenced by traditional Japanese house design.

was Wright's introduction of the kitchen as part of the open plan in his Usonian houses, beginning in the 1930s. Until this time, kitchens had been kept well out of sight, along with all the smells of kitchen preparation and cleanup. The advent of good kitchen ventilation technologies changed all that, and Wright was the first architect to take advantage of its benefits.

Varied ceiling heights are key

What made Wright's open-plan houses work so well was his use of architectural elements to differentiate one area from another, especially his use of varied ceiling heights. Without this variation, a house with an open plan can be pretty dull.

Because we are so focused on floor plans to evaluate potential living arrangements, we often forget to consider the ceiling as an element that defines our living spaces. You might think that 8-ft. ceilings are homogeneous and boring, but it's not so much the ceiling height as the fact that the height is the same throughout the whole space. This holds true for houses with all 9-ft. or all 10-ft. ceilings as well.

The key to making any open-plan house more interesting is to vary the ceiling height to introduce some distinction between

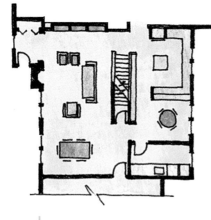

Defining space.
Even a humble open-plan ranch house benefits from ceiling variation. It adds visual interest and defines the rooms without using walls.

activity areas. It makes a world of difference without making any structural changes at all (illustrations above).

The open plan becomes the great room

Open plans seem to become more popular every year, and they do offer great benefits for the modern family: greater flexibility to rearrange functions and activities as the family grows and changes, better circulation, and more natural light.

But many new home designs favor very large rooms with ceiling heights to match, making it difficult to find comfort or a sense of home. The advent of the great room concept brought with it many houses with the kitchen right in the middle of the family living area—not an altogether bad idea, given our more informal lifestyles today. But what has caused a lot of problems in such homes is that, in order to avoid the 8-ft.-ceiling blahs, we've now gone to the opposite extreme and made these spaces overly tall but still with no spatial definition between activity areas.

The acoustics of such spaces can be a nightmare, especially when the TV is on, someone's listening to the stereo on the balcony overlooking the great room, and someone else is making dinner. All these sounds are magnified by the tall and undifferentiated ceiling surfaces. Again the solution lies in manipulating the ceiling plane, but you may also need to add some sound-absorptive materials and even a door or two to help soften and contain the noise.

Fixing an open plan that's too open

Changing ceiling heights in an existing house may seem to be a daunting and expensive project, but there are some fairly simple things you can do. Taking a common great room layout as an example (illustrations p. 20), here are strategies you can employ to keep the openness but increase livability:

- Lower the ceiling over the kitchen so that it becomes a more contained space. If the ceiling of the great room is really tall, you may even be able to turn the space over the kitchen into a loft.

- Create an implied ceiling over the eating area. This can be done at the simplest level with a hanging light fixture that suggests a lower "ceiling" above the table. If you want more definition than this, a hanging "cloud" made of anything from fabric to

wood-veneered plywood can help create a more sheltered eating area beneath. This same technique can be used over the living area, too.

- Add a surrounding soffit or display shelf just above window height. This helps to break up some of the sound bouncing around the room and also creates more of a sense of shelter for the activity below.

Many new home designs favor very large rooms with ceiling heights to match, making it difficult to find comfort or a sense of home.

Soaring spaces can make you uneasy. An overly tall great room with no spatial definition between functions (below) can be made more comfortable by defining spaces from above (right).

The open plan is definitely here to stay, and it has liberated us from the more formal constraints of separate rooms for each activity. But it's time to look back to the lessons of the original open-plan homes to make our great rooms work effectively and feel comfortable. With varied ceiling heights—and other elements that delineate one room from another—we can create boundaries around open spaces without resorting to solid walls, and our open-plan houses can be just as inviting and nurturing as the originals.

Let There Be Light

Daylight has a huge effect on the way we feel, both about our home and about life in general. As our houses have gotten bigger, more of our living spaces have moved away from perimeter walls and therefore away from natural light. But there are ways to enhance windows and skylights to make the most of the daylight they bring into the home. It's not as simple as just adding more glass area; rather, it's how you locate the glass in relation to walls and ceiling surfaces that really makes the difference.

Built-ins that bounce light

It would seem to make sense that if a room is on the dark side, you should add a window or skylight, but this may not be necessary. First, see if there's a way to make the light that's already entering reflect farther into the space. A simple way to do this is to add a shelf directly above the existing window or to frame the window with something I call a "wing" wall, which creates a reflecting surface immediately adjacent and perpendicular to the window (illustrations p. 22). As a result, the room appears to have more daylight and is therefore significantly brighter. In essence, you are using your wall

When adding windows or planning a house from scratch, I like to place the windows close to a reflecting surface to get the most daylight.

Borrow light from existing windows.
Add reflective surfaces adjacent to the windows to bring light farther into a room. At right, the bright light flooding in is in stark contrast to the wall surrounding the window. Below, a built-in bookcase, a shelf above the windows, and "wing" walls around them create a transition area that will reflect light and make the room appear brighter.

Consider windows before skylights

When it comes to adding windows and skylights, my rule of thumb is to start with the window as the solution of choice and to consider a skylight only if a window won't work. I have two reasons for this: First, light from a skylight is less controllable than light from a window. And, second, a skylight creates a penetration through the roof, which is the area with the greatest potential for heat loss and heat gain. Since glass, even with double or triple glazing, has a much lower resistance to heat flow than an insulated roof does, a skylight isn't the ideal way to let in light.

and ceiling surfaces as reflectors, just like the reflectors you find in a lighting fixture.

When you implement this strategy, you may find that you gain more daylight than you would have with the addition of several windows, and you'll save some money, too.

A window can be protected from the sun's direct rays in most situations, either with a wide overhang if the window is on the south side or with vegetation if the window is on the east or west side, where the sun's rays are at a lower angle. Plants or trees can provide protection from direct sun, creating a softer, more diffused light. Of course, interior shades and blinds are also effective. Controlling direct sunlight through windows is not as big an issue in cool locales as it is in hot climates, where a room can become uninhabitable when sunlight is streaming in.

Add windows where they reflect off adjacent surfaces

When adding windows or planning a house from scratch, I like to place the windows close to a reflecting surface to get the most daylight. Rather than putting a window in the center of a wall, I'll often place it adjacent to a sidewall so that the entire wall surface becomes a light reflector (illustration right). This placement not only increases the amount of usable daylight but also adds a wonderful softness to the room, because the light becomes dimmer the farther from the window it is.

Of course, there are times when it is most appropriate to locate a window centrally in a room. In such instances, consider allowing it to extend all the way to the ceiling. This way, the ceiling becomes the reflecting surface to increase the penetration of daylight into the space.

When skylights are a better choice

Sometimes a window can't be used, so a skylight is the logical choice. This was the case in my own home, a Cape Cod with steeply sloped second-floor ceilings that extended almost to the floor. Because one of the rooms I was remodeling was very dark, I added a skylight and located it adjacent to a wall so that lots of daylight could be bounced into the space, transforming a dark room into a light-filled haven (top illustration p. 24).

Place windows next to a wall or ceiling or both. Walls and ceilings are some of the largest reflective surfaces in your home. As long as they are painted a relatively light shade, windows adjacent and perpendicular to either will illuminate them, providing a gradual transition from light to dark.

In some places, only a skylight will do. It can be a challenge to shade a skylight from midday sun, but in an attic with a sloped ceiling, a skylight may be your best or only choice. Be sure to get a good-quality skylight installed by an experienced professional because proper sealing is crucial.

Skylights can also be an excellent choice in rooms where you need all the wall space for storage or in rooms where the view is not a priority, like a closet or a bathroom. Again, if the goal is to maximize the amount of daylight, locate the skylight near a wall so it can serve as a reflector.

In places where a skylight just won't fit, a solar tube (also known as a sun tunnel) is a good solution. A solar tube is a highly reflective shaft that leads from the roof surface to the space needing daylight. A diffuser on the ceiling helps regulate the light from the shaft so it's not just a single point of brightness. I use these in hallways, closets, and utility rooms where there's no room for a skylight shaft (illustration left).

Solar tubes brighten spaces where windows and skylights cannot. For hallways, bathrooms, walk-in closets, or places where a window or skylight is not practical, a solar tube can be the right solution. Best of all, solar tubes are affordable and easily installed.

Good natural light is important in our homes and workplaces. If you've ever had to work in an office without access to daylight, you know that your body can become lethargic and you end up feeling bored and uninspired by things that usually appeal to you. We are light-sensitive creatures, and despite advancements in artificial lighting, it's hard to beat real sunlight when it comes to physical, psychological, and spiritual health.

Where Does the Garage Belong?

America's homeowners have a love/hate relationship with their garages. While the garage can house one or more of our most expensive and prized possessions, it typically is a large structure that has little personality. And although there have been significant improvements in the design of the garage over the last few years, its location continues to be a point of discussion.

When the garage is the first thing you see, directly off the street, the whole house seems to shriek that the automobile is the most important thing in the homeowners' lives. A few years ago, builders started offering such front-of-house garages with three or more stalls. The roof that sheltered the garage often dwarfed the scale of the house. Builders quickly learned that buyers were turned off by this large appendage to the face of the house. In response, they changed designs to make the size and visual impact of garages less offensive, such as setting the third stall back a little and giving it a smaller-scale roof or making the garage side loading so that the doors didn't face the street.

There are many strategies that help to de-emphasize the garage. To find the best solution for your needs, consider the size, location, and style of the garage. Whether you are building

When the garage is the first thing you see…the whole house seems to shriek that the automobile is the most important thing in the homeowners' lives.

An unobtrusive garage tucked under the house. From the street, this side-loading garage does not dominate and allows the proper focus to be placed on the front entry.

new, remodeling, or dreaming about changing your garage, there are many ways to make it fit in with your house and the neighborhood.

How many stalls do you need?

Before you even think about where the garage should be located, you need to know how big it should be. The climate you live in, the number of vehicles you own, and your storage needs have an impact on garage size. For a single car and not much else, a 10-ft. by 22-ft. garage will do. At the other end of the spectrum is a veritable barn for a fleet of automobiles.

The two-car, 24-ft. by 26-ft. garage seems pretty typical in the South, where I live now,

although many people don't have a garage and don't seem to miss it. However, in Minnesota, where I lived for more than two decades, a house with anything less than a three-car garage can be considered undesirable. Because of extreme weather, parking outside means a half hour of hard labor every day in winter to clean off snow and ice.

In working with many homeowners over the past few decades, I've discovered that almost everyone uses a part of the garage for storage. One couple insisted upon a three-car garage, but when I went to visit them a few months after they'd moved in, I saw that all their cars were parked in the driveway, and the entire garage area was being used for storage. When I expressed surprise at this, they were surprised at my surprise. In their minds, that's what a garage was for. They'd never intended to store their cars there!

The point is that the placement of storage space doesn't require the ease of access from the street that a car does, so when you are planning your garage, identify the number of vehicles that need to have direct access in and out of the driveway. Then, if you want additional space for a lawn mower, a workbench, or extra stuff you don't want in the house, recognize that these do not need the same kind of access.

Determine the best location

Downplaying the garage from the front of the house can be done in a number of ways and will depend quite heavily on the characteristics of your lot.

If you have a lot with a long street face, you may have room to make the garage side-loading (illustration facing page). This puts the garage in a more appropriate relationship to the house and allows the house to look like a dwelling rather than a garage with a house attached.

With the right amount of space, you can have a detached garage or one connected to the house by a breezeway. Although in colder climates this may seem to be a disadvantage, in terms of indoor air quality, it provides complete separation between automobile exhaust fumes and the conditioned interior air of the house. Because of this air-quality benefit, many homeowners who build on larger lots select this approach.

There are also significant design advantages to having the garage in a separate building.

A garage designed with appropriate form and scale. Here, the garage doors are not seen from the street, so your eye reads the garage as part of the house. The repetition of the gabled roof form and the garage's smaller scale help it blend well with the house, without overwhelming it.

A front courtyard that also serves as a driveway.
When space is tight, you can place the garage at a 90-degree angle to the house and turn the driveway into an elegant and functional main-entry courtyard.

The garage can be located to define an entry courtyard or a garden space buffered from prevailing winds.

If space is tight, you may need to hire an architect to help find an appropriate spot for a garage. A Minneapolis-area neighborhood built in the 1920s had no alleys and no room for garages on the street. The solution: a narrow driveway down the side of each house with a garage either at the back of the lot or attached to the house. Unfortunately, for many developments and narrow lots, there's no other option than to place the garage on the street side of the house. If this is your situation, consider turning the garage in relation to the house so that it is perceived as a subordinate wing rather than as the most important feature of the front façade. If you have the depth of lot, you may even be able to turn the garage at 90 degrees to the street

so that the doors aren't facing the street at all. Both of these approaches create a sort of courtyard for the home that can significantly enhance the sense of entry as well (illustration above).

Dress up the façade

If the doors must face the street, then spend a little extra on the doors themselves, to make them a more personal expression than the typical panel or metal door. Custom garage doors are more expensive than their off-the-shelf competitors but definitely worth it in terms of enhanced house character. However, if you have a tight budget, consider a high-density fiberboard door and add a few pieces of trim to give it personality. Almost any variation from the standard will help to distinguish it and make it less obviously a garage door.

Changing your existing garage doors is an effective and inexpensive way to create a better-looking garage. For example, in illustration no. 1 below, a standard wood-panel door has been modified to bring the two side glass panels down below the center ones, giving the door a more graphic character that greatly improves the look of the house. The other illustrations offer more options.

Whatever the challenges facing you with respect to the garage, keep in mind that the front of the house is essentially your statement to the world about what's important to you. As more people realize that they don't want to be known for the predominance of the automobile in their lives, our house designs will become better.

Simple changes to standard garage doors can make a big difference.

1. Instead of four windows in a row, try four in a square. Many garage door companies are willing to make these types of modifications.

2. A standard, flat garage door can be dressed up with 1x4 or 1x6 wood trim. Paint the panels and trim in different colors to add personality.

3. Many custom and semi-custom garage door companies are returning to traditional designs. Explore your options.

4. Design something to match a motif that appears elsewhere on your house. This type of design can easily be applied to a front door or roof gable to add continuity.

TWO

Room by Room

Today's homes are used very differently than they were 50 years ago. We live much more informally than we used to, so a house built even three or four decades ago is generally ill-suited for the way we live today, often with walls and cabinetry separating rooms that we would rather have connected. There are also rooms that rarely get used, such as the formal dining room and guest bedroom, that could serve some other function in addition to the one the room is named for. To fix these problems, it's time for a blueprint that's designed to reflect our current lifestyles rather than that of our parents and grandparents.

At the core of this blueprint is a rethinking of the formal spaces, rooms that generally sit empty, waiting for a type of guest that stopped showing up a long time ago. Now when we have friends over, they want to spend time with us in the parts of the house we live in every day. Gone is the need for the pretense of formality.

But it's not just the formal spaces that need updating. It's also the informal spaces, like the everyday eating area and the kitchen, which serve different functions than their earlier purely functional incarnations. In fact, as you'll read, the kitchen is now the hub of the house and the launching pad for most household activities. Reworking the floor plan of an older home to acknowledge the way we really live may be the most important act we can make to update the house for the lives it now accommodates.

And then there are the rooms that we've only recently begun to recognize the need for, like the away room and in-home office, rooms that can contain and acoustically protect an activity requiring privacy or quiet from the more active and noisy gathering spaces.

This is not an exhaustive list of all the rooms in the house, but you'll learn as you read how to think creatively about every space, opening each one up to others where connection is desired and providing a means of containment where more privacy is preferable.

As our activities within our homes change, it's important to regularly check that no spaces are sitting idle too much of the time or are decorated in a way that makes them unworkable for the functions they're intended for. This kind of critical thinking can help to keep your home current with your present-day lifestyle.

The New Heart of the Home

In days gone by, the hearth—the brick or stone-lined fireplace used for heating and sometimes cooking—was the heart of the home. It provided warmth in the winter and a central focus for household activities throughout the year.

Today, with central heating and built-in ovens, we no longer need that same kind of hearth. A fireplace may provide a primal connection to simpler times or evoke powerful memories of past events, like gathering around the campfire or getting together at grandmother's house for the holidays. But it's no longer a necessity and no longer the central gathering place it used to be.

. . . the kitchen has replaced the fireplace as the focus of most homes today.

When it comes to house design, we often become attached to a solution. Then we continue to build that solution into every house for centuries after its true utility has passed. This is what happened with the fireplace. It transformed from highly important element to nostalgic accoutrement without our even noticing. But the need for a place to gather together as food is being prepared is still an important part of our lives. It's time to reassess what a hearth really is today and to find the center of the place we call home.

Where's the center of *your* home?

It's clear that the kitchen has replaced the fireplace as the focus of most homes today. It's where food is prepared and often eaten. It's where household members pack up the things they need for their day and then unload them 12 hours later. If there's a party in the house, it's where most people prefer to hang out, and if friends come over, it's where they'll most likely be—amidst all the activity.

But why is this so? Many homeowners, and especially the cooks among them, complain about their inability to keep their kitchen work area free of extraneous bodies, yet this is nearly impossible. It's human nature to want to be in the middle of the hubbub, and since food preparation is such a regular and engaging activity, the kitchen is the location of choice in most homes. Rather than trying to keep guests and family members out, what about designing a kitchen that welcomes them in, as did the hearth of yore? Instead of assuming that the hearth is synonymous with the fireplace, let's start over. Let's design a hearth that's truly the heart of the home—one that nurtures the soul, not just warms the body.

How do people gather in your kitchen?

Kitchen design today focuses on cooking and storage. Making room for visitors is barely considered, even though it's most likely one of the primary functions of your own kitchen. In many kitchens, people park themselves around the work area, leaning on countertops and cabinets that offer a good place to perch. In other kitchens, there's a peninsula or island with two or three bar stools (almost never comfortable) that provide a place to sit down but still seem to emphasize the temporary nature of the visit

Raise the upper cabinets. Upper cabinets between the kitchen and dining area can present a visual barrier to communication (left). Raising or even removing them allows the cook to make eye contact with people on the other side of the counter.

rather than the opportunity to settle in and get comfortable.

If there's an informal eating area close to the kitchen work space, this can be a more satisfactory gathering place, but often these spots are either too far away from the work area to function properly as a hearth or they're separated by a visual barrier that makes communication awkward despite the proximity. If you can't look directly into someone's eyes as you are speaking, he might as well be on the other end of a telephone line.

A family room that's open to the kitchen may appear at first glance to offer a perfect hearth, but as with the eating area, if the distance between it and the kitchen is too great, people won't congregate there unless they are engaged in a separate activity, such as TV watching.

Some solutions for today

What's needed is a small sitting area adjacent to the kitchen that welcomes family and friends to gather comfortably as food is being prepared. Such sitting areas became popular features in kitchen designs a few years ago, but with our inability to judge appropriate proportions, they were often made too big and too far away from the kitchen work surfaces to serve as an extension of the kitchen proper.

For such gathering places to be successful, they must be designed to keep the distances between functions to a reasonable minimum, so communication between cook and kitchen visitor can be unencumbered by the room's design. Gathering places that work include the following options.

■ One alternative to the uncomfortable bar stools lined up at a counter is to design an eating alcove within a small kitchen (left illustration facing page).

Move people closer to the kitchen. If the family room is too far away, the cook can feel isolated. Here, a small, informal table and chairs and a seating area focused on a woodstove provide cozy gathering places close to—but not in—the kitchen.

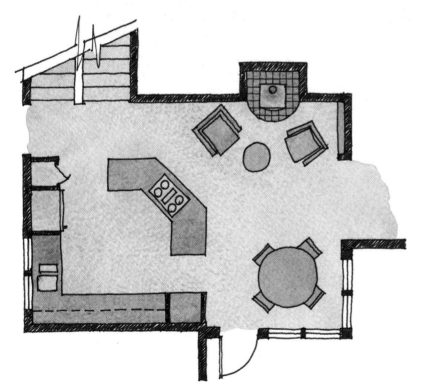

Trade the bar stools for an eating nook.
Sitting at a bar is often uncomfortable (below), but a built-in nook, especially if it has a window, is snug and inviting. And it still allows the cook to have company—away from the work area.

- A solution to visual barriers is to eliminate or open up overhead cabinets so the cook and guests can make eye contact with one another (illustrations p. 33).

- An alternative to the too-distant family room is to design a small seating area directly adjacent to the kitchen (illustration facing page). The plan shown here even includes something that might conventionally be called a hearth—the woodstove.

For today's households, think beyond what was once a necessary element of homes, like the fireplace or woodstove, which has now in many cases become only a seasonal need or decoration even. While you can certainly include a fireplace in your design— or even an inglenook for that matter—think of the new hearth as the gathering place itself and you'll be building in a type of warmth that lasts all year.

Rethinking the Informal Eating Area

The informal eating area is one of the most heavily used spaces in most houses today, yet its design often leaves much to be desired. Although informal dining isn't a complicated function to design for, proportion and ambience are key to its success. These aspects, though, are most commonly botched.

It always has seemed odd to me that the spaces we live in the most get short shrift, while the spaces we use once or twice a year are given the best views to the outdoors, as well as most of the decorating dollars. We've all been in homes where the informal eating area is in the least desirable space on the main level yet is the focus of much of the family's social time. What a difference it can make if the eating area is close to windows, with views to a garden. Combine this prime location with thoughtful proportioning and surrounding finishes, such as walls, built-ins, and lighting, and the room easily can be made to fit the functions it serves to a tee.

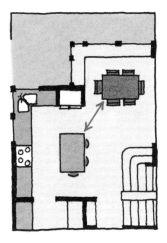

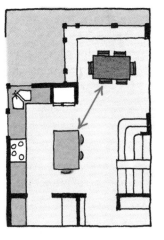

A few feet make all the difference.
Although the kitchen/eating area on the left looks more spacious, the relationship at far left works far better. Someone sitting at the table is close enough to the cook to be able to engage easily in conversation. In the plan at right, the table is essentially in a different room.

Design the room for its uses

To design any room, you first must determine what its uses are. The following are the most common functions of an informal dining space:

■ Drinking coffee and reading the morning paper

■ Eating meals with the family

■ Doing homework

■ Paying bills

■ Gathering with guests

■ Playing games

■ Sitting and chatting with the cook while dinner is being prepared

■ Hanging out, individually or as a family

With a little extra care in design, the room also can serve these additional functions:

■ Dining on more formal occasions or for holiday gatherings

■ Setting out a buffet during parties

Proximity to the kitchen

With many of these functions, proximity to the kitchen is paramount, so it's no surprise that almost all informal eating areas are adjacent to the kitchen. But anyone who has made a study of these spaces knows that many eating areas are a bit too far from the kitchen to work effectively. The informal eating area can't

What a difference it can make if the eating area is close to windows, with views to a garden.

be more than a couple of strides away or it won't be used. Many people can observe this phenomenon in their own home: They have an unused eating area because they belly up to the kitchen island for meals on the run. They assume it's because they prefer the bar stools at the island. Move the table and chairs just a few feet closer, though, and suddenly everyone's using them.

So while it's good to give the informal eating area a little differentiation from the kitchen with a dropped ceiling, perhaps, or a change of flooring material, the addition of too many lineal feet between the two turns it into a less-than-ideal area that doesn't serve its intended function (illustrations facing page).

I designed the eating area in my own kitchen so that I would be able to lean back from my chair at the table and get water from the refrigerator's water dispenser. This feature quickly became a favorite, and it ensured that the table was not too far away from the kitchen. Any farther away, and the space would have been much less a part of the kitchen and more formal as a result (top illustration p. 38).

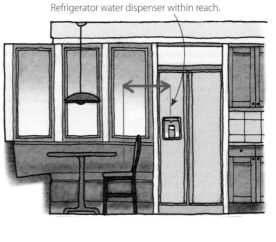

Refrigerator water dispenser within reach.

My kitchen.
For an informal eating area to work well it should be closer to the kitchen than you may imagine. Here, I can lean back in my chair to get water from the refrigerator, a great convenience and an indicator of appropriate proximity.

A blocked view is no connection. Many houses have the proximity between the kitchen and the eating area correct, but cabinets above a peninsula block easy access and sight lines. Reorganizing the layout as shown on the right dramatically improves flow and visual connection.

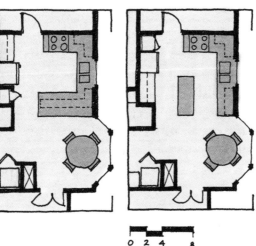

0 2 4   8

Remove obstructions to the view between kitchen and eating area

If you are remodeling an older home, you may have a kitchen/eating-area arrangement with good proximity but also with a row of upper cabinets above a dividing peninsula that obstructs the view between the two rooms. Remove the cabinets, and you may find that the space works wonderfully, with only minimal remodeling. If there's a soffit (a dropped ceiling) supporting the cabinets, you may want to consider removing that, too, if it creates too much of a psychological barrier.

In a recent remodeling project, I oriented a kitchen to create more usable counter space and to increase the sense of flow between kitchen and eating area (bottom illustration left). Although the eating area had a lot to recommend it, with an adjacent bay window overlooking the backyard, upper cabinets above a peninsula made it essentially a separate room. With an island to replace the peninsula and the removal of the soffit, the proportions of the space were ideal.

Cooks who worry about the view to a messy kitchen may prefer a peninsula with a slightly raised back. The cook can converse with those at the table, but work surfaces are obstructed from view. If it's easy for people to make eye contact without having to duck down or crane over an obstacle, then the arrangement works.

Make it a wonderful place

When designing an informal eating area, make sure that the place is beautiful, that it takes advantage of a view to the outdoors, and that it's a pleasure to sit in. Spend your extra decorating dollars here, where you can enjoy their effects every day rather than in areas of the house you rarely use. Adding some special touches, such as wraparound windows, extra trim work, or built-ins and paneling, can make this place something delightful.

You also may want to take advantage of a special feature of the site. Some people, for example, love to sit in a sunny spot with their morning coffee. If this is a daily ritual, place the eating area on the east side of the house. Perhaps there's a particularly beautiful tree that you'd like to be able to see frequently. Orienting the eating area to take advantage of this view creates a strong connection between inside and out, and reminds you daily why you chose this piece of land.

Design for the holidays

One further consideration is to design the eating area so that it can expand to accommodate holiday gatherings and parties. Although we typically think of the formal dining room for such occasions, the formal dining table is where many families lay out the buffet. Guests, however, take their plates to the family room to eat. A better solution is to make the informal eating area serve this function so that it is closer to the family room, the guests' final destination.

You can make the table in the eating area the place to set out the food, or—my favorite

solution—you can design the table so that it can be extended to seat many people (illustration below). With some thought early in the design process, this setup is not difficult to arrange and may eliminate the need for a formal dining room altogether.

When something is designed beautifully, we use it automatically. It fits the functions we need it for without making us feel awkward or uncomfortable. It is often said that the kitchen is the most important room in the house, but I suggest that the informal eating area is at least as important, if not more, because for many households today, it's really the heart of the social space.

Give the table room to grow. If you plan to use an eating area for formal and informal occasions, you can design the space to allow the table to extend into the family room with only minimal furniture rearrangement.

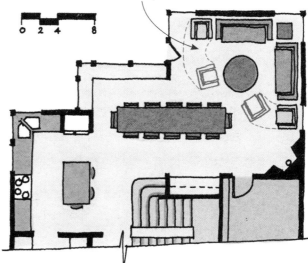

Move chairs back when table is expanded.

o 2 4 8

Rethinking the Formal Dining Room and Living Room

It always amazes me to discover homeowners who consider adding on without assessing whether their existing space is being used effectively. It is far less expensive to find a new use for a room than it is to build an addition. But because we tend not to explore the alternatives for infrequently used rooms, they sit dormant most of the time. By looking closely at the most commonly underused rooms—the dining room and the living room—you might find that much-needed space is there already.

The formal dining room

If you are attached to your dining-room table and chairs, any alternative functions for the dining room need to include this furniture. What often stops people from changing the use of the dining room is the fear of scratching the tabletop, but a table-surface protector can be purchased from any household-supplies catalog.

Many of the households I've worked with have a much-loved collection of books and magazines with no permanent home. Many of the books are still in boxes from the last move, and piles of magazines are stashed

> *It is far less expensive to find a new use for a room than it is to build an addition.*

Think of it as informative wallpaper.
Lining the walls of a formal dining room with bookshelves can turn it from a room that's used only at Thanksgiving to one that the family visits daily.

in odd corners. In households with such bibliophile tendencies, my favorite design solution is to line one or more of the dining-room walls with shelves (illustration above). This simple change makes the dining room a highly functional library, with every volume easily visible and accessible, and with a perfect reading surface—the table—at the center of the room.

If you subscribe to several magazines, consider some dedicated shelves that include storage space for back issues and display space for recent issues (illustration p. 42). Combined with bookshelves, this approach nets a room that's decorated with a most vibrant wallpaper.

Not only does adding books to the dining room give it a warm, inviting atmosphere,

Create a home for your favorite magazines.
A built-in such as this one puts current issues in view and keeps past issues organized and readily accessible.

Because most houses lack a set place for both activities and because mail often ends up on the dining-room table, why not make it official and design the room for these functions?

Instead of bookshelves, you may want to line one or more walls with integrated file cabinets and mail-sorting slots (illustration facing page), along with a spot to keep a laptop computer. If these things aren't aesthetically appropriate when you have guests to dinner, you can always design them with a sliding door or roll-top cover to hide the offending piles. For bill-paying, the table surface provides plenty of layout space, and the bills, along with past invoices and receipts, can all be close at hand.

Another set of uses for the dining room becomes possible if you don't have a table and chairs to accommodate. If your family takes meals only in the informal eating area, the formal dining room can be used for a variety of other purposes. It can be turned into an excellent away room: a place to be away from the hubbub of the family room or to isolate the noise of video games, for example. Or it can be used for the cook, who can split his or her time between both rooms, preparing a meal and handling the day's business endeavors at the same time.

Clients often express a wish for a hobby room or craft space, and again, the dining room's location adjacent to the kitchen makes

but it also offers household members the opportunity to engage in some quiet activity away from the TV and other goings-on. For children, the dining room can serve as an excellent place to do homework. Because most dining rooms are close to the kitchen, a parent is usually within earshot if assistance is needed, but the room is secluded enough to minimize distractions.

No books? Consider a mail triage center

If you're not a bibliophile, two other tasks readily accommodated by the formal dining room are mail-sorting and bill-paying.

it an excellent candidate for such activities. Either a counter surface running along the perimeter of the room or a good-size work-table in its middle can provide plenty of layout space. Because crafts usually have a lot of equipment and supplies associated with them, you also might consider covering one wall with shelving, cupboards, and/or drawers.

The formal living room

Three primary reasons explain the underuse of formal living rooms: uncomfortable furniture, lack of visibility from the activity hub of the house, and duplication of function. The first is easy enough to solve but not always obvious until it's pointed out. If you have decorated the living room for looks alone or have designed it around inherited furniture that gives the room a stuffy formality, chances are you rarely use the room. In this case, the rare use of the room has nothing to do with its shape or location but everything to do with what you've put in it. If you want a room to be used, make it comfortable and functional. Family members need to feel welcome in the room, and some everyday activities, such as listening to music, reading, or watching television, need to be accommodated there.

Because most formal living rooms are separated from the kitchen, they are often out of sight and mind. The simple act of opening a wall between it and the kitchen, which is typically the center of household activities, results in the living room being used more (illustration p. 44).

Typically what stops people from opening up a wall is lack of knowledge about the structural properties of interior walls. Even

Pay bills here. Come the end of the month, formal dining rooms with big tables provide plenty of space to spread out invoices and the checkbook. Built-in files along the wall provide easy access to needed records.

Without a visual connection, forgetting a room is easy. An opening in the wall between a kitchen and a formal living room can turn the latter seldom-used space into a family favorite.

room with a different function altogether. I've helped quite a few households turn these rarely used spaces into excellent home offices. Especially in situations where clients come to the house, formal living rooms can be ideal as conference spaces or counseling rooms. Separation from kitchen and family room in this case becomes an asset rather than a deficit.

Once you think beyond conventions, you may find all sorts of things you can accommodate in your own home. I've had clients turn their unused spaces into painting studios, exercise rooms, and greenhouses. Although you are using the room in an innovative way, it doesn't preclude a future owner from returning it to its original function. In my experience, though, once those future owners see what you've done with an outmoded room, they'll be more inclined to think outside the box themselves.

with a bearing wall it's usually relatively easy to make an opening in it without compromising the integrity of the structure. You simply need to hire someone, like an architect, builder, or remodeler, who can help appropriately size and install the header for the opening.

For many households, though, there's no need for a second sitting area. The family room provides for both family and guests. So the formal living room can be turned into a

Designing an Away Room

The away room is a newcomer to the stable of rooms that constitute a house. It was invented to solve a common problem in homes: dueling noises. Whether the battle is TV vs. conversation or stereo vs. video games, household noise can disturb even the most focused family member. In many houses, it can be difficult to find a place that isn't filled with either human or electronically generated sound.

Therefore, with noise as motivation, the away room was born. This new addition is a small space where one of two things can happen: A door can either confine noise to or block noise from the away room. You actually can design the away room to serve both functions. For example, when the clanging of pots and pans makes it difficult to hear the 6 o'clock news, a TV in the away room can be used. When a movie is being viewed on the away-room TV, someone not interested in the film can move to the family room to read or listen to music.

Where to put an away room

One of the keys to the effectiveness of the away room is to position it properly for your household. For most, an away room works best if it opens directly off the family room through a French door. Because young children generally follow their parents around, there's little likelihood that younger children will use either room independently. Older kids, however, will be able to make significant noise (which, of course, is their tendency) in an away room without creating a disturbance. The visual connection afforded by French doors will keep older children from feeling cut off while allowing parents to monitor their children's activities (top illustration p. 46).

> *Whether the battle is TV vs. conversation or stereo vs. video games, household noise can disturb even the most focused family member.*

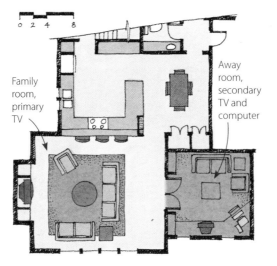

Family room, primary TV

Away room, secondary TV and computer

Location, location, location. Positioning the away room adjacent to the living room or kitchen keeps families close together while effectively containing noise. French doors block unwelcome sound and provide a clear sight line for a visual connection that allows parents to monitor children.

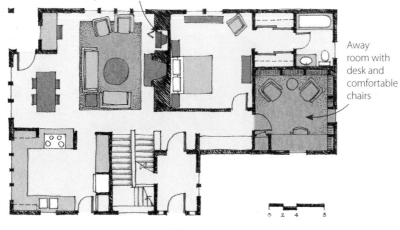

Only TV in house

Away room with desk and comfortable chairs

The away-room retreat. A more remote away room increases the separation between people and noise. The room becomes a retreat where family members can get away to engage in quieter activities such as reading or homework. A closed solid door can act as a "Do not disturb" sign.

If the away room is intended as a retreat for adults and older children, a location farther away from the main living area may be more appropriate. A more isolated location creates an escape where family members can find greater privacy and acoustical separation. Someone using the away room in a house arranged in this fashion, however, may be perceived by the rest of the family as absent from family activities. In some households, this is normal and acceptable while in others it is not, so the location of the room should reflect the needs and personalities of the particular household (illustration bottom left).

The nature of the door

We rarely stop to think about how powerful a message a closed door sends. If the door to the away room is solid, closing it sends a clear signal that the person within doesn't want to be disturbed. On the other hand, when the room's user doesn't want to send such a strong message and leaves the door open, the acoustical value that inspired the room in the first place is greatly diminished. For that reason, my preference is to use a double French door where possible. This type of door maintains the visual connection and softens the message sent by a closed door while continuing to block noise.

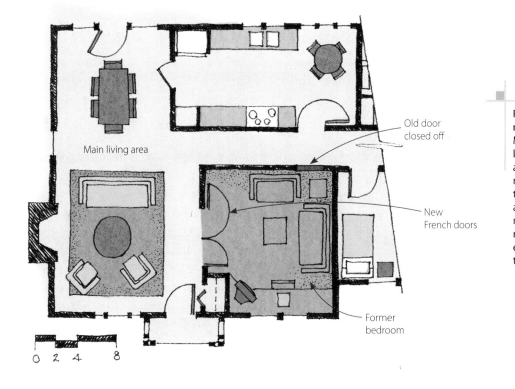

Main living area

Old door
closed off

New
French doors

Former
bedroom

0 2 4 8

Remodeling for an away
room is often simple.
Many ranches and bunga-
lows are well suited to
accommodate an away
room with little construction. If the living area abuts
a bedroom, the transfor-
mation may be as easy as
repositioning the room's
entrance from the hallway
to the common area.

Remodeling to add an away room

Away rooms are not exclusive to new homes. In many older homes, an existing room can be converted to an away room with only slight remodeling. Although it is typically accessed through a hallway, a bedroom adjacent to the living room is common in ranches and bungalows. Adding a pair of French doors to the wall separating the living room from this bedroom and closing off the door opening in the hallway converts the bedroom into a perfect away room with an ideal location (illustration above).

Some homes have a rarely used dining room. Fitting a pair of doors in the dining-room opening transforms the existing space into a useful away room. You can decorate the room for a designated purpose or leave it as a dining room with the table serving as a desk. The result is a great place to pay bills, talk on the phone, or read. While the space remains a dining room, the doors allow it to serve alternative functions with greater acoustical privacy.

Designing the away room

Once the location of the away room has been determined, its size, character, and layout must be considered. Away rooms don't

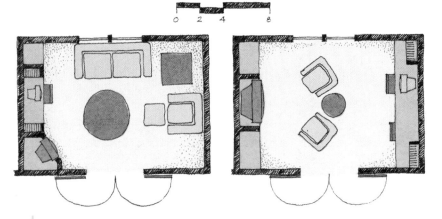

Design the room for the family's needs. Away rooms can be planned for designated activities, function as a multiuse area, or double as a second family room. While the layout on the left is ideal for watching TV, using the computer, paying bills, and reading, the one on the right is more specifically arranged for video gaming and browsing the Web.

need to be large and will be more welcoming if their scale contrasts with the adjacent room. In new homes, I usually size away rooms at 11 ft. by 15 ft. However, a smaller room works fine. Start by listing the activities that could occur in the room. If the room is to serve as both a retreat and an activity area, some functions may duplicate those that take place in other rooms. The following is a list of activities that could be accommodated:

■ Video-game playing

■ Internet browsing

■ Talking on the phone

■ TV watching

■ Studying

■ Reading

■ Playing with toys

■ Paying bills

■ Listening to music

Next, determine the furnishings you want in the room. If the primary function of the room is a secondary TV area, you'll want to make sure that seating is comfortable and that the TV is centrally located. Other activities can take place in a small alcove along one wall. If, on the other hand, the main purpose of the room is to contain video gaming, you may want to consult the video-game users about ideal layout. Do they prefer to lie on the floor, with the screen lower to the floor than would be typical for standard TV watching? Or would it be better to have desk chairs in front of a large TV monitor that would also be convenient for surfing the Internet? If you make a list of priorities, you'll see which activities should influence design. If you want to monitor children's activities, make sure sight lines to the main activity areas are unobstructed.

Away rooms negate the need for the multitude of single-use rooms that are becoming increasingly common. With more efficient use of space, houses can be smaller, giving family members a greater sense of connection. This versatile room eliminates common noise issues and increases overall household harmony without confining anyone to the far reaches of the house.

Designing a Comfortable Guest Room

Over the years, I've stayed at many people's homes and have become a connoisseur of guest bedrooms. Sad to say, the vast majority offer guests a less than pleasant experience. Because we tend to be overly polite when staying in someone else's home, though, this information rarely is passed to the homeowners.

Spend a night in your own guest room once or twice a year to make sure it provides the comfort you want for your guests.

You can avoid this problem by spending a night in your own guest room once or twice a year to make sure it provides the comfort you want for your guests. A noisy furnace fan or lack of space to leave a suitcase can make a guest's visit far from enjoyable. Designing a room that is welcoming and stress-free requires planning. Here are a few considerations to maximize a guest's chance of a comfortable stay.

The nature of guests

Guests come in many shapes and sizes. They can be people you know extremely well, such as family members, or people you barely know, such as business associates. A young niece may have no qualms about sleeping on a futon on the floor, but the same experience may debilitate Grandma for weeks. Designing for the most physically challenged guest you expect to accommodate is important. The nimble niece

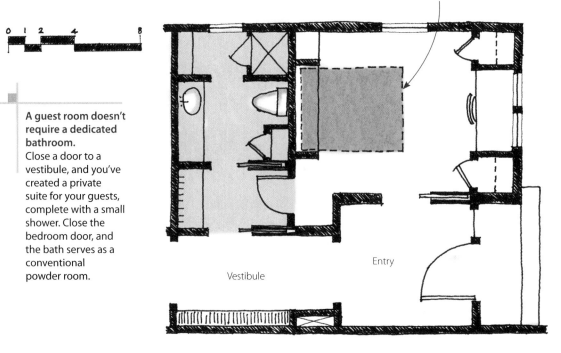

Fold-down bed allows home office to convert to guest room.

A guest room doesn't require a dedicated bathroom. Close a door to a vestibule, and you've created a private suite for your guests, complete with a small shower. Close the bedroom door, and the bath serves as a conventional powder room.

Vestibule

Entry

won't be put out by the extra comfort, and Grandma will be truly appreciative.

Locating the guest room

I strongly recommend locating the guest room away from the family's sleeping rooms. This arrangement affords both guests and family members a respite from each other's company and minimizes awkwardness when retiring or getting up in the morning. Everybody can go about their standard bedtime or morning rituals without worrying about disturbing others' habits.

It's also important to locate the guest room so that guests don't have to traipse through family living areas to get to a bathroom. Having to pass through primary living spaces to get to the bathroom can make guests uncomfortable. On more than one occasion, I've waited silently in the guest room until all family members are in bed before creeping through the family room to the bathroom they've designated as mine to use.

It's usually not necessary to build a bathroom devoted to the guest bedroom. One of my favorite solutions is putting the guest bedroom on the main level, which is easily accessible to elderly visitors, and placing it adjacent to the powder room. In these cases, I usually tuck a shower around the corner so that the room appears to be a conventional powder room (illustration facing page). If the powder room is given a vestibule that can be made private to the guest bedroom, visitors have a personal suite, and you won't have the expense of an extra bathroom.

If your home has a dry basement, the guest bedroom can go there. This arrangement is obviously not good if you are likely to have mobility-impaired guests, however.

Although basement bedrooms can be private, other issues often make them unpleasant. Many lower levels are significantly cooler in winter than the main and upper levels. Without insulation under the concrete slab, floors throughout feel cold to the feet. Typically, the furnace lives in the basement, and it can generate significant noise (illustration right). For some reason, guest bedrooms are frequently immediately adjacent to the furnace room. The noise of the furnace clicking on and running over the course of a winter's night can make sleep all but impossible. I have taken to traveling with earplugs to minimize this problem, but infrequent travelers can enter such a room and be guaranteed eight hours of misery.

Bedroom practicalities

The guest bedroom is typically provided with the same storage as the other bedrooms in the house, perhaps a 5-ft. to 6-ft. closet and some sort of dresser. But a guest's needs are different from those of residents. Guests usually have a suitcase or two, but often, there is nowhere except the floor to open them. They have a bath sundries kit and no place to put it and a bathrobe but no place to hang it. Typically, the closet is full with no room for the few garments that guests would like to hang up.

Don't place the guest room next to the furnace. Although basement guest rooms tend to be more private, if they're adjacent to the mechanical room, a restful night's sleep can be all but impossible.

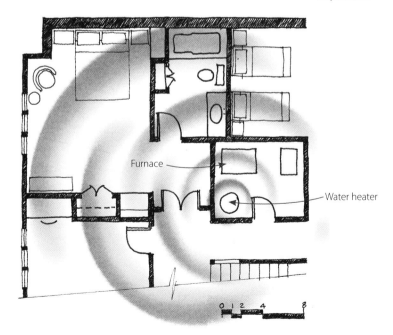

Furnace

Water heater

0 1 2 4 8

Guest-room closets can be significantly smaller than standard bedroom closets because only a few items need to be hung. But suitcase layout space is important. My favorite solution in this situation is to provide about 3 ft. of hanging space in the closet and then 4 ft. of flat space on which to open suitcases or a built-in dresser (illustration facing page). Add three or four hooks for hanging things on pegs rather than on hangers. And provide a chair in the room for those guests who don't hang up clothes.

You may not need window coverings in your own bedroom but your guests will. Many people can't sleep once the sun comes up and lights the room, so a shade or drape that cuts all light is a necessity. And even though you as the homeowner may know that no one outside can see into the guest-bedroom windows, your guest doesn't know that. It can be disturbing for someone who is security conscious to have no window shade.

As for actual sleeping comforts, make sure the mattress is in good condition, that the bed doesn't squeak when you turn from one side to another, and that the covers afford comfort for a variety of body temperatures. A single down comforter with a sheet beneath may look beautiful from the bedroom doorway, but it's impractical for guests who overheat easily since they'll be too hot with the comforter on and too cold with only a sheet. Providing a readily accessible blanket is an easy remedy.

And don't forget about the pillows. Some like down, but others are allergic to down. Some like their pillows well stuffed, while others like a lower-loft option. And some always sleep with two pillows. Providing a couple of different types of pillows—even if they're hidden from view on the closet shelf—can make an immense difference to your guest's quality of sleep (and demeanor the following day!).

It's important to locate the guest room so that guests don't have to traipse through family living areas to get to a bathroom.

Guest-room closets differ from those in other bedrooms. A surface on which to open a suitcase is a great convenience. About 3 ft. of closet for hanging clothes is sufficient, and a hook or two close at hand are helpful.

Guest bathroom practicalities

Because guests usually tote a bag of bath sundries, it's important to provide a place for both the bag and its exhumed contents. If the sink is not surrounded by countertop, then provide a shelf close by. Guest bathrooms rarely have enough hooks and towel bars. I suggest at least four hooks and two good-size towel bars. A nonslip surface or rubber mat for the tub/shower is also critical for older guests, and fabric bath mats are important, especially if the floor is often cold. Few things are less hospitable than feet on a cold floor as you prepare for bed or as you rise in the morning.

Testing it out

Now that you think you've thought of everything for your guests' comfort, spend at least one winter night and one summer night in the room. Take note of what sounds occur over the course of the night.

The sound made by some familiar-to-you piece of equipment may be disturbing to guests. Even if you can't cure the noise, you can at least let them know what it is. You might even put some earplugs in a drawer by the bed.

Most of us focus on our guest room's decor, but true comfort includes livability and functionality as well. Understanding and designing for your guests' true needs can make their stay at your home a delight and make you into the appreciated host you intended to be.

THREE

Attention
to Detail

To make your home all it can be, both functionally and aesthetically, it is important to attune your senses to the small details that make everything look and feel perfectly integrated into the design of the house as a whole. This is not generally a field of consideration that garners much attention in the house-planning process, and yet it is perhaps the most important quality in differentiating an average home from a truly stellar one.

When I refer to "detail" I mean those design features that are woven right into the fabric of the structure and finish work and give the home its personality. They are apparent before you move in any of your belongings. It is the integration of each element of construction into the overall composition that makes us ooh and ah. Without the careful attention to those small details, however, the experience of the house is ho-hum at best.

So how do you pay attention to detail? This section will give you pointers for a variety of details that can make a positive impact upon the house as a whole. We'll start with some related to proportioning—an issue that is commonly overlooked. When something doesn't look the appropriate size to our eyes, we have the distinct impression that the whole house is insubstantial or too big or too small to be comfortable. How often have you driven past a house where the columns holding up a deck or porch roof look like toothpicks rather than the substantial load-bearing members that our eyes know they should be? And how many houses have you visited that have rooms that feel either too tall or too short for the size of space? A 12-ft.-high powder room can feel a bit like an elevator shaft, while a large living room with an 8-ft. ceiling can make you want to crouch. In each case the proportions are wrong, and a little attention to detail is needed to fix the problem.

We'll also look at how to seamlessly integrate some of the required electronic and built-in mechanical features of a modern home. If these are left to the builder's discretion, nine times out of ten you'll be disappointed with the results. But if you learn how to put your desires on the blueprints, you can save yourself substantial heartache and frustration without any additional cost.

Column Proportion: Bigger Is Usually Better

Proportion is tricky to write about because it's based on what looks—and feels—right. The way building elements (doors, windows, roof, etc.) look together dictates how we respond to them: We know something's right or wrong but we're not sure what or why.

In designing houses, we have in the past relied on traditional models of proportion. For example, in building a colonial house, a model developed over centuries specifies the size and shape for building elements. These relationships established the proportions, which remained unquestioned for decades, and any deviation from the traditional model occurred only occasionally; as a result, styles evolved very slowly. (For a wonderful reference guide to these traditional styles and proportions, check out *Get Your House Right* by Marianne Cusato.)

Solutions beyond the traditional

Home design today is based less on traditional models than it was in the past. Houses now take on all sorts of new forms. Sometimes these houses are designed beautifully with pleasing new forms, but, more often, they look like a soup of miscellaneous shapes and proportions. Although many homes attempt to imitate

Accurate scale drawings allow your eyes to decide…whether the column is the right size.

Narrow columns look fragile and flimsy. Drawing a detail at a larger scale can help you evaluate what looks best.

Bigger is better. Although the porch itself is a gracious design feature, the skinny columns detract. With more substantial columns, the porch becomes an asset because all the parts are in proportion to one another.

traditional and vernacular styles, the appropriate proportions are frequently botched. Nowhere is this more apparent than in column size.

We've all seen decks that appear to be supported on toothpicks. They look as though a strong gust of wind would blow them down. Although the support is structurally sufficient, our eyes tell us otherwise—it doesn't matter what a structural engineer says.

But how do you choose a pleasing width for columns? As a rule of thumb, when working with the exterior of a home and building

57

Beefed-up columns support visually and structurally.
These 4x4 columns (below left) look like they will bend in a high wind. Even though the columns are structurally sound, our eyes tell us otherwise. In contrast, 8x8 columns make a big difference visually. The deck looks solid, and the columns appear substantial enough to carry the load.

> *When working with the exterior of a home and building with wood, take the size of the structurally required member and…double it.*

with wood, take the size of the structurally required member and at the very minimum, double it. If a 4x4 is all that's needed, use an 8x8 or larger column. This rule may seem wasteful, but it improves the character and curb appeal of a home immensely. If you take a careful look at many older homes in inner-ring suburbs, you'll actually see columns that are 12 in. to 14 in. square. They are often tapered from bottom to top to give a graceful elegance to the form, which a straight column lacks. Another way to achieve this sturdier-looking result is to use two smaller columns side by side, giving the effect of a wider one.

You can use the same doubling multiplier on the interior of a house as well, though here you can get away with less without it looking as odd as it does on the exterior. Instead of a 4x4 here, you could choose anything between a 6x6 and an 8x8 for a one-story column. Many people will automatically choose the narrowest column possible on the interior because they're worried about blocking views between rooms. But unless you have a very contemporary design and are using metal columns, the narrow version can look awkward and insubstantial. Bigger in this case is almost always better, even for a Not So Big house or remodeling, and the worries about blocked views are largely unfounded. If a column is in the way, we move, and barely even notice it's there. We often forget that the column is in fact what has allowed the removal of a far bigger obstruction—a wall—and is defining the edge of a room or activity area as an implied space divider.

To make practical use of this doubling rule, do what architects do: Draw a couple of pictures. We don't know the right answer until we've drawn it a few times and compared the results. Accurate scale drawings allow your eyes to decide with certainty whether the column is the right size. After experiencing this certainty, you'll see that it's the quickest, easiest way to figure proportion.

Computer programs that allow you to see designs three-dimensionally—and from the viewers' height—give the most accurate feedback of all. But if you aren't adept with any of the 3-D programs now available to help homeowners visualize, a two-dimensional drawing of the area you're studying also gives an accurate picture.

So the long and the short, or should I say the thick and the thin, of it is that you should beef up those columns. Wide, chunky columns look much less odd than narrow, spindly ones.

Interior columns define a space. These narrow columns (left) are more than adequate structurally but look proportionally insubstantial. Doubling their size makes the columns appear more appropriate to the opening and surrounding casework.

Unifying an Interior with Horizontal Trim

When I was in architectural school, I fell in love with Japanese design and spent hours poring over the details of Japanese house and temple architecture. Later, I found out that several of our culture's favorite architects, including Frank Lloyd Wright, the Brothers Greene, and Gustav Stickley, to name a few, did the same. If you look back at the architecture of the Arts and Crafts movement and the Prairie School, you'll see the unambiguous markings of Japanese influence: the horizontal bands of natural wood trim, usually with no other shaping or embellishment, that run continuously above windows and doors; the varying ceiling planes, their heights controlled by these horizontals; and the ganging of windows to create bands of long horizontal views for their inhabitants.

As I practiced my craft in the ensuing years, I realized that we had much to learn from these masters about how the spatial qualities of a house designed in all three dimensions, height included, can be enhanced with the use of trim work. Over the years I've developed a set of simple trim application principles that can help turn almost any home into a spatial delight. The following suggestions show different approaches—a less expensive version, a middle of the road version, and a more expensive version. All three require a bit more finish carpentry than a house without these features, but the results are well worth the added cost.

The horizontal trim band takes precedence over vertical trim lines.

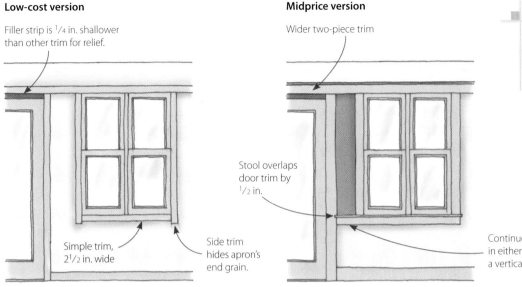

Low-cost version

Filler strip is 1/4 in. shallower than other trim for relief.

Simple trim, 2 1/2 in. wide

Side trim hides apron's end grain.

Midprice version

Wider two-piece trim

Stool overlaps door trim by 1/2 in.

Continue apron and stool in either direction until they meet a vertical trim piece.

The tallest opening determines the height of the trim band. Window headers all should be at the height of the tallest door to determine the height of the horizontal trim band. A filler strip bridges the gap between shorter doors and the horizontal band.

Don't jog the trim around windows or doors. A change in trim height looks like a mistake.

Whether you are remodeling or building new, these strategies can give a character to the whole composition of the home that many people respond to positively when they experience it firsthand. Although these elements generate a particular style of design, their practice can help all of us to become more adept at designing in all three dimensions rather than just extruding the floor plan upward until it runs into the ceiling or roof plane.

Use uninterrupted horizontal trim above doors and windows

A primary horizontal trim band is the identifying feature in a Prairie style or Arts and Crafts style house, and I use the same strategy for my trim application principles. The horizontal trim band takes precedence over vertical trim lines.

Effective use of this band takes some planning because you must install all door and window headers at the same height. If you have different-height doors, install the trim line at the height of the tallest opening and add a filler strip between the flanking verticals (illustrations above). This single, uninterrupted height gives the interior a sense of continuity as you move from room to room, whether you are in a utility room or in the living room.

Use the trim line as the height for dropped ceilings or soffits

Lowering the ceiling height in smaller spaces, such as window seats and alcoves, creates a tailored look that provides a sense of shelter. When I employ this technique, I like to rest the soffit on top of the trim line. For a more sheltered feel, you can align the bottom of the dropped ceilings with the bottom of the trim line so there's no head trim at windows and doors, but this generates some tricky details at doors beneath the soffit, where any shift in the structure over time will cause the door swing to hit the ceiling directly above. The solution here is to raise the height of the trim line at least 1 in. above the height of the tallest door and to use a filler strip to bridge to the soffit as I do when a door height is shorter than the base of the trim band. (You can see a similar condition in the photo on p. 60, where the upper cabinets have a spacer added above to avoid hitting the surface of the soffit.)

Use butt joints instead of miters and vertical casings at corners

If you look closely at Japanese interiors, you'll notice that wherever two pieces of wood come together, they always are butted, a key characteristic of the Arts and Crafts movement as well as the Prairie School. This technique works well when you butt door or window trim into the continuous head trim. However, the bottom of the window can present a problem. Although I don't mind exposing the end grain of a piece of trim at the window aprons, this look bothers many people. To avoid any displays of visible end grain, you can run the side trim down past the apron, or you can run the apron all the way across the room in either direction until it meets a piece of vertical trim (see Midprice version illustration p. 61 for an example of this).

> *To avoid any displays of visible end grain, you can run the side trim down past the apron, or you can run the apron all the way across the room in either direction until it meets a piece of vertical trim.*

Low-cost version

Main ceiling

Soffit

Window

Soffit height at the bottom of the trim band provides the most sheltered feeling.

High-cost version

Light cove

Soffit

Horizontal trim on soffit and below soffit

Lower ceilings in small spaces make the area more comfortable.
Establishing the ceiling, or soffit, height at the top of the trim band allows for elaborate trim treatments, while using the bottom of the trim band for the ceiling height offers an even more sheltered feel. Adding casing to corners is a nice finishing touch.

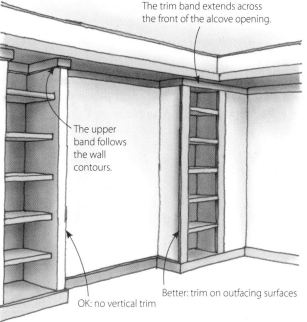

The trim band extends across the front of the alcove opening.

The upper band follows the wall contours.

OK: no vertical trim

Better: trim on outfacing surfaces

Wherever there is an alcove, an opening into a hallway, or a set of recessed shelves, cased openings look more finished and are easier to maintain than untrimmed openings, which tend to get scuffed and marred in the course of everyday living. The wood provides a far harder surface that's much less likely to be damaged. If you trim these openings like a doorway, with trim on all the exposed surfaces (illustration p. 64), be prepared for a substantial increase in the cost of the project.

That many lineal feet of trim can add up in a hurry. The advantage, however, is that you don't need to use wallboard corner beads, and the house will look pristine and new for decades.

A less expensive alternative is to apply trim only to outfacing surfaces. For a cleaner look, use trim wider than the wall to match the width of the baseboard wrapping around the corner.

Horizontal trim provides the organizing principle.
Bands of horizontal trim provide the organizing principle for the rooms in a house by defining the heights of windows, doors, ceilings, and soffits. This room shows the most elaborate, and most expensive, version of the organizing principle of horizontal trim, with multiple horizontal trim bands as well as a liberal use of trim to case all outside corners.

Use secondary horizontals to add another layer of detail

I often add a lower horizontal trim band in bathrooms at the height of the vanity backsplash or countertop. A backsplash that stops at the edges of the vanity looks odd in a house emphasizing horizontal continuity. By running the trim line at the room's midsection, there's a place to attach towel bars as well as a line to stop tile surrounding the bottom half of the room, another detail that can add significant cost. If you look at bathrooms in Arts and Crafts bungalows, you'll notice many of them sport this detail.

I also use secondary lower trim lines in any room where budget allows and where the windows all sit at the same height off the floor. This gives the space a tailored look and draws attention to the lower section of the room, making it ideal for areas like the window seat on the facing page.

Avoid abrupt endings and jogs in trim height

The art of making this aesthetic work is to watch for places where the continuity is likely to be disrupted and design to accommodate this condition (illustrations p. 61). In other words, it should be one of the first considerations in your decision-making about trim-band heights. The key is to make

Trim helps us see the variations in heights of spaces, adding to the delight of the spatial experience.

every trim line continuous. A jog in height will look like a mistake. If a window or two are below the designated height required to fit neatly below the trim line, extend the jamb trim to the continuous band and add a filler strip.

Although these "rules" may seem picky, they can make a house look both cohesive and beautiful—at least if you like continuity and order. It turns out that many of the architects of the Arts and Crafts movement and Prairie School were doing more than teaching us the style they practiced in. They were also shaping the third dimension—the heights of everything—and defining the variations in heights with trim. This is the underlying reason why their architecture holds so much appeal.

Just as makeup accentuates and defines facial features, trim helps us see the variations in heights of spaces, adding to the delight of the spatial experience. Just as we were given a grid to practice with when we were learning to write, these trim lines are giving us a grid of sorts in which to perceive the art of three-dimensional perception.

Fixing a Room That Is Too Tall

There are literally millions of homes built in the last three decades that have a surprising problem that seldom gets discussed—ceilings that are too tall for the area of the room they shelter. Bringing a too-tall space down to more human proportions can dramatically improve the functionality and the character of not only the room in question but also the entire house.

Too-tall ceilings come in all sorts of shapes and sizes, from the cathedral ceiling, with proportions reminiscent of their namesake, to flat ceilings that are 10 ft. to 12 ft. above the floor—which is all very well when the room is 30 ft. by 30 ft., but not at all comfortable when it's a breakfast nook or powder room. Most people who are saddled with such a problem find themselves largely avoiding these too-tall rooms because of the feeling of discomfort that accompanies them. But there are some simple solutions that can make that rarely used floor space significantly more comfortable to be in and thus more frequently used.

The ideas that follow are just a few of the possible solutions. A local architect or interior designer will be able to help you evaluate which is the best solution for your situation.

Use a line of horizontal woodwork or moldings around the walls to define the upper part of the room.

Add some visual weight

The simplest and least expensive solution is to paint the ceiling a dark color. When a surface is dark, we perceive increased visual weight, which makes the ceiling seem

A darker ceiling brings a room down to size. Painting the ceiling a dark color is inexpensive and a great way to make the ceiling feel heavier, giving the room a more intimate feeling.

Trim marks the new top of the room. Add trim, and the ceiling seems to extend down to it. Painting the upper and lower areas different colors reinforces the separation of the two parts of the room.

heavier and therefore closer to the ground. A coat of darker paint will make a remarkable difference at a relatively low cost.

As with any paint color experimentation, test colors first on a piece of plywood or wallboard that's at least 4 ft. by 4 ft., and hold it in place against the ceiling to make sure you like the color before you commit to it. This will save you significant aggravation when you discover that you've picked a color you don't like very much. Color is never easy to get right the first time around.

Add a line of wood trim

Another option is to use a line of horizontal woodwork or moldings around the walls to define the upper part of the room (illustration above). The trim is usually located in line with the top of the window, also called the window head. If there are transom windows above the main windows, you can use the height of either window head for the trim line's location, which I refer to as the head band.

To further distinguish the upper and lower parts of the room, you can paint the area above the head band, together with the ceiling surface, a different color from the area below the head band. This technique works best when the two colors selected are quite different from one another, either in saturation or hue. Your eye senses the area above

A soffit allows for more comfort and light. The addition of a soffit creates a sense of shelter around the edges of a room and makes even the center of the room feel more comfortable. Soffits also make an excellent place to locate recessed lighting, which emphasizes the area below it.

the head band as the "lid" of the room below. It doesn't matter whether the area above or below is the darker one—each way creates a different effect, and both will make the room seem more comfortable to sit in.

Add a soffit

Lowering a narrow section of ceiling— what architects and builders refer to as a soffit—can help a room feel more welcoming. By adding a soffit that's 2 ft. to 3 ft. deep along one or more walls of the room, you can bring the vertical proportions of the room down to a more human scale. This technique gives the center of the room a greater sense of intimacy, even though it is still at the original height.

The right height for the bottom of the soffit depends upon the proportions of the room, so it's difficult to generalize, but I'd recommend locating it somewhere between the height of the top of the highest windows and 1 ft. below the ceiling. The lower you can make the soffit within this space, the more impact it will have on the perceived height of the room.

Incidentally, soffits make an excellent place to locate recessed lighting, which further emphasizes the area of the room below the soffit height in the evening hours.

Add a surrounding shelf

If you like the idea of creating a lowered edge to the room but high windows prevent you from installing a soffit, then you can use a floating shelf instead. The shelf can run along a wall or around the entire room at the height of the main or upper window head. This provides a visual break between the upper and lower sections of the room. As with the other techniques, you are focusing attention on the area below the shelf, fooling the eye into believing that the shelf is the top of the room. Even though it is obvious that this is not so, a far greater sense of shelter is given to the entire room.

You can create a similar effect with a linear segment of wood lattice, which is especially useful where there are tall windows. By locating the lattice between upper and lower windows, you will be gifted with some delightful shadow patterns when direct sunlight streams through.

Make one room into two— one up, one down

The last, and most obvious, solution, if you have a very tall space, is to divide it vertically into two rooms. There are many cathedral-ceilinged rooms that would be greatly improved if they were remodeled in this way. As they are often 18 ft. or more tall at the ridge, the only time they don't seem so overwhelming is when the house is being used for a party and there are plenty of people to fill up the space. Although these rooms look impressive in a photograph, they just don't work well for one or two people sitting and having a conversation or watching TV. Their height makes them echoey and inhospitable.

When divided into two, you not only gain space for another activity but you also create two new spaces that feel more intimate and livable. The new ceiling height of the lower room can be made to match that of its surrounding space, and the upper room will have a sloped ceiling that will give it a cozy, cottage-like feel—a rarity in homes like these.

Often it is possible to provide access to the upper room from an existing stairway, but if the floor plan does not allow this, then you can add a spiral stairway, which will make it feel like a crow's nest on a boat—an ideal play space for kids, a tucked-away retreat, or an in-home office.

If you rarely use an existing too-tall room because it's uncomfortable to be in, then it's essentially wasted space. Use any one of these techniques to reclaim your room and make it a valued and more useful part of your home.

A shelf lowers the perceived ceiling height. Not only does a shelf make the ceiling seem lower, but it also acts as a display place. And if you have a very tall window, instead of the shelf, use a lattice that crosses the window.

Improving a McMansion with Ceiling Height Variety

I often get asked by the owners of large, amorphous suburban houses if I have any suggestions for them that will help them make their "not so SMALL" dwellings a little better proportioned for everyday living. Several years ago I decided to take on a couple of these McMansion retrofits and in the process came up with a simple ceiling height hierarchy "by the numbers" approach for these types of remodelings. This

For best results, hire a good architect or designer to help you bring "too bigness" back into balance.

is by no means the only way to bring "too bigness" back into balance, but it is a simple approach that will allow you to do some of the design work yourself if you want to.

For best results though, I recommend hiring a good architect or designer to help you. Here's the process:

1. Take the floor plan of your house and **identify the main gathering places**. Indicate the existing ceiling heights of each, as well as the window head heights. If there are two sets of windows, one above the other, in some rooms, make a note of the head height of the lower set of windows as well as the higher set.

2. Indicate with a dotted line any places on the floor plan where a second-floor platform stops and a two-story space begins. This is an existing ceiling height hierarchy that you'll need to keep in mind as you develop your new ceiling height plan (illustration facing page).

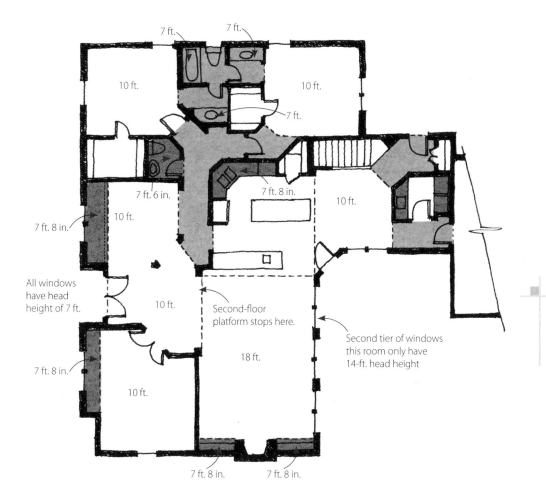

7 ft.

7 ft.

10 ft.

10 ft.

7 ft.

7 ft. 6 in.

7 ft. 8 in.

10 ft.

7 ft. 8 in.

7 ft. 8 in.

10 ft.

All windows have head height of 7 ft.

10 ft.

Second-floor platform stops here.

18 ft.

Second tier of windows this room only have 14-ft. head height

7 ft. 8 in.

10 ft.

7 ft. 8 in.

7 ft. 8 in.

Identify activity areas.
This McMansion originally had 10-ft. ceilings throughout except in the great room, where the ceiling height was 18 ft. The first step in identifying places where ceiling heights could change is to mark the natural separation lines between activity areas with dotted lines and then to shade in hallways and alcoves.

3. On your floor plan shade any **hallways and alcoves** in a different color. This is easier, though more time-consuming, with a computer program, than a pencil or colored marker, but the time it takes will be well spent because it will allow you to preview in two dimensions the ceiling height hierarchy you are developing (illustration above).

4. Now look for natural separation lines between activity areas that aren't divided from one another by walls. Show these division points with a dotted line as you did in step 2.

5. At this point, it is useful to make some copies of your plan thus far. You'll be sketching over these as you try out different ceiling height alternatives. If you prefer, you can use sheets of tracing paper laid over your original plan instead.

6. Your next step is to **decide on a height for the hallways and walkways**. You can go as low as 7 ft. if you have standard 6-ft. 8-in. doors. As a rule of thumb, I'll use 7 ft. if the main ceiling heights throughout the house are at 8 ft. And I'll use somewhere between 7 ft. 6 in. and 8 ft. if the main ceiling heights are 9 ft. or higher. It isn't so much the exact height that is critical,

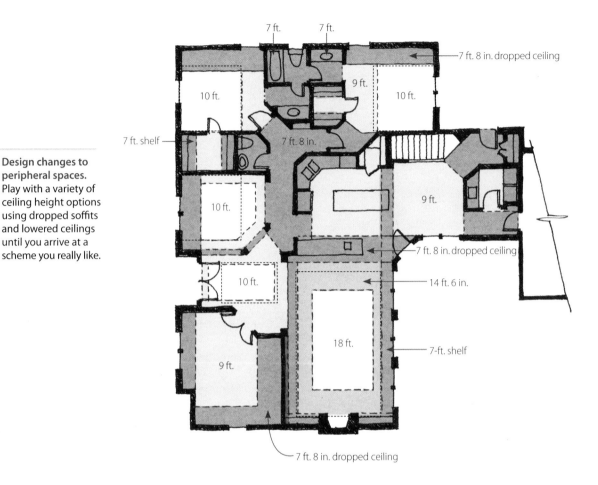

7 ft. 7 ft.

7 ft. 8 in. dropped ceiling

9 ft.

10 ft. 10 ft.

7 ft. shelf

7 ft. 8 in.

Design changes to peripheral spaces. Play with a variety of ceiling height options using dropped soffits and lowered ceilings until you arrive at a scheme you really like.

10 ft.

9 ft.

7 ft. 8 in. dropped ceiling

10 ft.

14 ft. 6 in.

18 ft.

7-ft. shelf

9 ft.

7 ft. 8 in. dropped ceiling

but that you use the hallways to provide a contrast in height with the spaces they are leading to.

7. Now you are ready for a little design work. Try extending a dropped soffit around one or more of the main living spaces at the same height as the hallways (photo p. 70). Shade in the proposed soffits using the same color that you used for the hallways. This color, as you'll now understand, is being used to indicate a particular plane of ceiling height. If you are dealing with a space that is very tall, you may want to create a higher soffit for this space and use

the lower soffit for peripheral spaces (illustration above).

If you are considering running a soffit around a room with two tiers of windows, you'll realize that a soffit in these windowed areas won't work because it will cover up the upper set of windows; a floating shelf may work well, however. The floating shelf will run along the mullion between the upper and lower windows and may need to be slightly lower than the hallway ceiling height if the window head height is at the standard 6 ft. 8 in. off the floor.

8. If you want to **look more closely at the impact your design idea will have** on the space, take a photograph of the window wall in question and draw the floating shelf onto the photo to see what it looks like, or draw the interior elevations for each space, as in the illustration right. This is a type of drawing that architects often use to study how ceiling heights will relate to one another in three dimensions.

9. Next, identify some of the **subordinate spaces to the main gathering areas**. In many homes, the kitchen and informal eating area will fall into this bracket. They open onto the family room, but they are smaller spaces and thus are subordinate in scale, even though in many homes they are the busier areas. These spaces can be given a third height if you'd like, or they can be made the same height as the hallways. Don't make a whole room 7 ft. tall. This height is fine for an alcove, but for a whole kitchen it would be oppressive.

10. Before you settle on a final scheme, try several different versions. If you have a computer-aided design program, you may actually be able to model the various ceiling height hierarchy ideas you are considering to see which one you like best. If you can't decide, just pick one. Any ceiling height variety is better than none, and in most cases there really is no best solution.

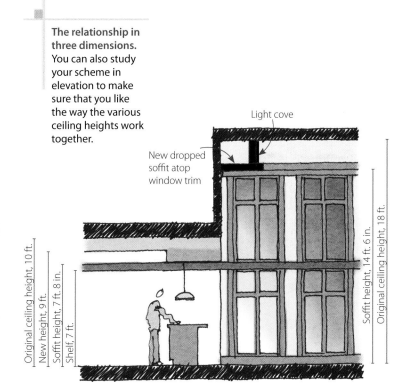

The relationship in three dimensions. You can also study your scheme in elevation to make sure that you like the way the various ceiling heights work together.

Light cove

New dropped soffit atop window trim

Original ceiling height, 10 ft.

New height, 9 ft.

Soffit height, 7 ft. 8 in.

Shelf, 7 ft.

Soffit height, 14 ft. 6 in.

Original ceiling height, 18 ft.

Although you can't easily make a "too big" house smaller in square footage, by implementing some of these ceiling height changes you'll be imbuing it with some Not So Big features that will help bring it back down to size visually. Ceiling height variety is very much like adding seasoning to food. If the seasoning itself is flavorful, the food it is added to will be tastier as a result. And if the ceiling heights selected are appropriate, the rooms they are added to will be more comfortable.

Making a Zero-Clearance Fireplace Look Real

A zero-clearance fireplace is an amazing product. Prefabricated from a metal box with a masonry lining, a zero-clearance fireplace can be found in both gas-fired and wood-burning versions. Either version is lightweight enough to be installed anywhere in the house, without a foundation or an expensive masonry chimney. Zero-clearance units are also substantially more energy efficient than the real thing because they burn hotter, so they more completely burn the fuel and polluting by-products. And just to top it off, they're significantly less expensive to install, making them more appealing than a conventional masonry fireplace to many homeowners.

However, this kind of fireplace, if not carefully integrated into the room in which it is destined to reside, can look fake. The chal-

Zero-clearance units are lightweight enough to be installed anywhere in the house, without a foundation or an expensive masonry chimney.

The basic box: a typical zero-clearance fireplace

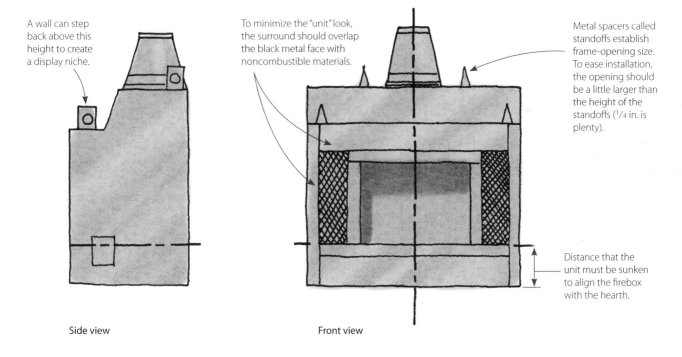

A wall can step back above this height to create a display niche.

To minimize the "unit" look, the surround should overlap the black metal face with noncombustible materials.

Metal spacers called standoffs establish frame-opening size. To ease installation, the opening should be a little larger than the height of the standoffs ($1/4$ in. is plenty).

Distance that the unit must be sunken to align the firebox with the hearth.

Side view

Front view

lenge is to make it look like the real thing. Over the years, I've developed a number of techniques that result in a well-proportioned disguise of a prefabricated fireplace unit, making it nearly indistinguishable from a real brick fireplace to all but the most discerning of visitors.

Zero-clearance units look most realistic when they have a minimum amount of brass on the exterior, when there is only a small amount of the telltale black metal box show-

ing around the firebox opening, and when the floor of the firebox aligns with the floor of the room. If you prefer a raised hearth (top illustration p. 78), align the firebox with the hearth instead. In either case, the result will look much more like a built-in masonry fireplace. To accomplish this alignment, the distance between the base of the unit and the firebox floor must be determined and the floor framing or hearth framing located accordingly.

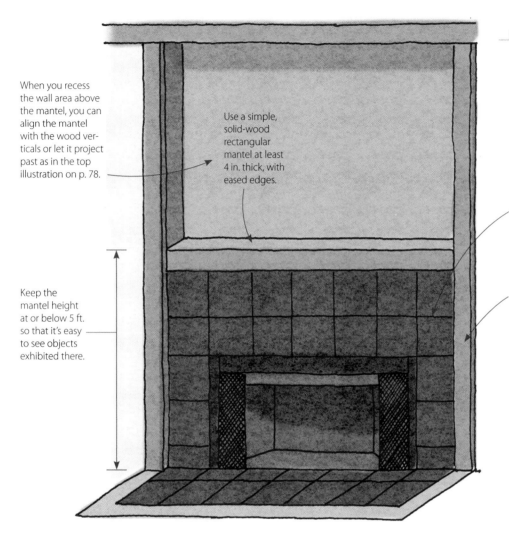

When you recess the wall area above the mantel, you can align the mantel with the wood verticals or let it project past as in the top illustration on p. 78.

Use a simple, solid-wood rectangular mantel at least 4 in. thick, with eased edges.

Keep the mantel height at or below 5 ft. so that it's easy to see objects exhibited there.

Flush hearth. Flush-hearth units blend in more effectively than surface-mounted units. This makes them seem more like a masonry fireplace.

A variation of the raised-hearth surround on p. 78, the two rows of 12-in. tile above the fireplace opening give a slightly more imposing look.

If you use a wood border around the tile, continue this border around the floor tile as well, making it flush with the tile surface.

Flush hearth

By recessing the zero-clearance unit into the floor, it blends in more effectively than if you were to set it directly onto the floor framing, which leaves the bottom of the firebox floating above the floor surface. Our eyes know this isn't the way a real fireplace looks. Although recessing the firebox requires more care and forethought during the construction process, it makes the unit look a lot more like a masonry fireplace.

There are many traditional fireplace surrounds available to choose from, but I prefer to use a simple, solid-wood rectangular mantel at least 4 in. thick, with eased edges, and I try to give the whole composition a three-dimensional quality. It is a common

One final detail that ties everything together is to continue the lines of the two vertical walls to either side of the wall inset down past the edges of the tile surround and onto the floor.

mistake to place the mantel at a height above the floor that is too tall for the proportions of our human bodies, which tends to make the fireplace too imposing for the room—fine for a large, stately mansion perhaps, but not exactly homey. I recommend keeping the mantel height at or below 5 ft. so that it's easy to see objects exhibited there.

By recessing the wall segment above the mantel, you can align the edges of the mantel with the vertical sidewalls of the inset and create a dramatic, sculptural composition that becomes a focal point for the room. Another alternative is to let the mantel project past the vertical sidewalls, as in the top illustration p. 78. In either case, by painting the wall inset a contrasting color from the other walls of the room, you will be giving it some visual weight, making it an ideal focal wall for hanging a special piece of artwork. The addition of a recessed light above can make the whole composition the clear center not only of the room in which it's located but also of the entire house.

If I am using tile as the noncombustible surround material, I prefer to use full rather than cut tiles if at all possible for a more tailored look; so after picking the tile and the fireplace unit I plan to use, I will lay out the design on paper to make sure that I can get the look I want without having too much of the black firebox showing. Some less-restrictive noncombustible materials are

marble, granite, and slate, which can be cut to the exact size you want. I usually aim to leave no more than 2 in. showing and preferably much less.

One final detail that ties everything together is to continue the lines of the two vertical walls to either side of the wall inset down past the edges of the tile surround and onto the floor, creating a border for the hearth tiles, as indicated in the illustration facing page. With my love of wood, I like to cap the vertical walls with wood and use a continuation of this wood border on the floor as well. You can accomplish the same alignment with tile if you prefer. It's the consistency of material and the alignment that create the effect.

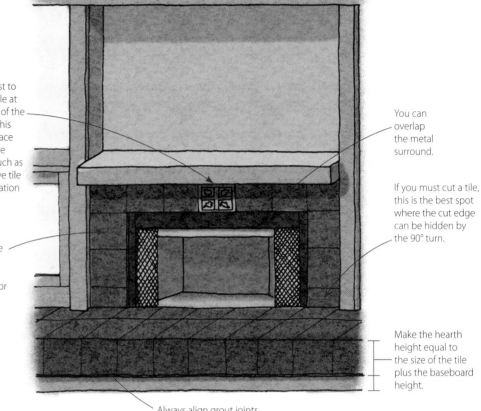

Raised-hearth surround.
A raised-hearth surround can disguise the unit. A built-up hearth should be high enough to allow flush adjustment with the floor of the firebox and should be of the same tile as the wall surround.

It looks best to use a full tile at the center of the fireplace. This is a nice place for a feature element such as a decorative tile or combination of tiles.

Select a tile size that eliminates the need for cut tiles.

You can overlap the metal surround.

If you must cut a tile, this is the best spot where the cut edge can be hidden by the 90° turn.

Make the hearth height equal to the size of the tile plus the baseboard height.

Always align grout joints between the floor and wall.

Fire codes determine hearth dimensions.
Codes vary from state to state regarding dimensions from firebox to combustible materials. One good look is a 12-in. tile (or stone) surround flanked by a wood post that stands proud of the tile. A 12-in. tile surround and up to a 1¹/₂-in. projection of wood should be legal in most states.

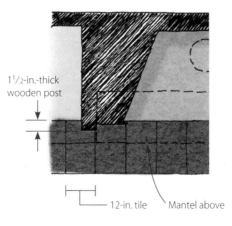

1¹/₂-in.-thick wooden post

12-in. tile — Mantel above

Raised-hearth surround

If recessing the unit into the floor is impractical or if you prefer having a hearth to sit on, a built-up hearth can disguise the unit in a similar manner. The hearth should be high enough to allow for flush adjustment with the floor of the firebox. I also like to cover the hearth in the same material as the wall surround. If you are using tile, be careful to align the grout lines of the tiles in the surround with those on the hearth to make the composition look its best. I like to make the hearth height fairly low so that it's easy to sit on. A good rule of thumb is to make it equal to the size of one or two tiles plus the baseboard height, but not taller than 16 in. off the floor.

It looks best to use a full tile at the center of the fireplace. This is also a great place for a feature element such as a decorative tile or a combination of tiles, as shown in the top illustration facing page.

Contemporary style

For a more contemporary look, you can recess the entire unit by 2 in. and use this as the primary design expression for your fireplace composition. Granite, slate, or marble provide a sleek look for the surround. I recommend making the top piece span the entire width like a lintel above a doorway and letting the side pieces appear as supports descending to the floor. If dollars are tight, you can even just paint the drywall instead of using stone for the surround. That's the beauty of this style. The focus is on the simplicity and elegance of the related parts, not on the materials per se.

Because a contemporary home is clearly nontraditional, there is less necessity for making the floor of the firebox align with the floor. We aren't comparing it in our mind's eye with what we know a standard masonry

fireplace should look like. If you are using a gas-burning unit, another more common approach in a contemporary home, you won't even need a hearth or noncombustible flooring surface in front of the unit, but if you do decide to include a hearth, be sure to align it with the edges of the 2-in. recesses, as in the illustration above.

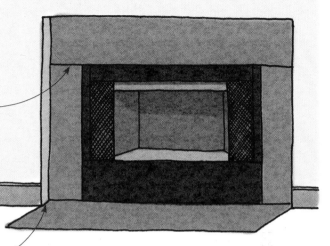

If you use stone or granite for the surround, make the top piece span the entire width like a lintel above a doorway and let the side pieces appear as supports descending to the floor.

The edge of the hearth and the edge of the surround always align and are both made of the same material.

2-in. recess

Contemporary style.
For a contemporary-style fireplace, recess the unit by 2 in. and use this as the primary design expression. You can use stone or granite as a surround, or for an even more contemporary (and less expensive) expression, use painted drywall.

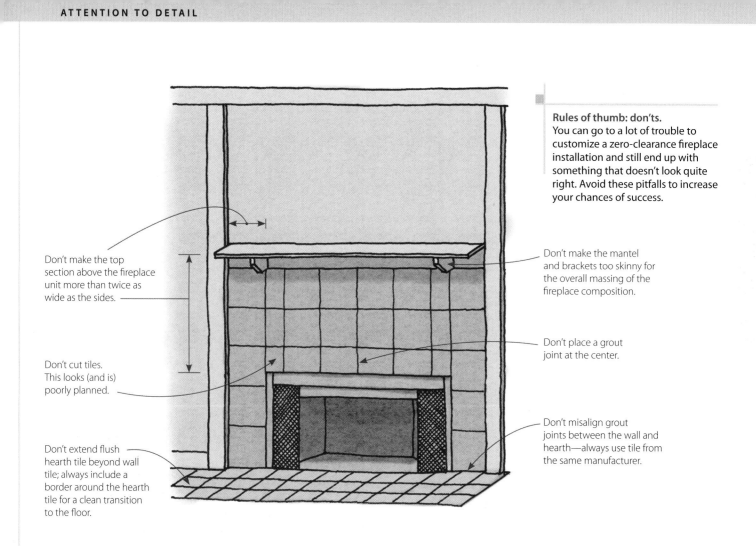

Don't make the top section above the fireplace unit more than twice as wide as the sides.

Don't cut tiles. This looks (and is) poorly planned.

Don't extend flush hearth tile beyond wall tile; always include a border around the hearth tile for a clean transition to the floor.

Rules of thumb: don'ts.
You can go to a lot of trouble to customize a zero-clearance fireplace installation and still end up with something that doesn't look quite right. Avoid these pitfalls to increase your chances of success.

Don't make the mantel and brackets too skinny for the overall massing of the fireplace composition.

Don't place a grout joint at the center.

Don't misalign grout joints between the wall and hearth—always use tile from the same manufacturer.

Make sure the materials used align in a pleasing way and that both the wall and floor surfaces are thought of as a singular composition.

No matter what your preferred style of surround, make sure the materials used align in a pleasing way and that both the wall and floor surfaces affected by the fireplace installation are thought of as a singular composition. This will make the fireplace look as though it is real and built just like the fireplaces of yore. But yours won't have cost nearly as much to install and will be much more energy efficient than any masonry fireplace will ever be.

Locating Smoke Detectors and Security-System Sensors

In an effort to make our lives more secure and safe from both fire and vandalism, we've filled our homes with a bevy of life-saving devices—from code-required smoke detectors to home security systems, which include sensors as well as their own smoke alarms. If you, your architect, or your builder are not paying careful attention, these often not-so-lovely units will end up being placed in odd locations during the electrical rough-in phase of the construction process, only to be noticed during finishing when relocation is likely to be expensive. A few simple guidelines can keep a beautifully designed room from being besmirched by an ill-placed smoke detector or security-system sensor.

Smoke detectors

The increased number of smoke detectors required by today's building codes has dramatically reduced the number of fire-related deaths, but it has introduced a design element often overlooked during construction. In addition to code requirements and practical considerations for locating each detector (away from the toaster in the kitchen, for instance), there are definite aesthetic concerns as well.

In a recent project, I changed the shape of a bedroom ceiling to add symmetry. I centered a light fixture on the new arched section of the ceiling, but I forgot to specify the smoke-detector location. The device was plunked in a convenient section of ceiling in terms of wiring, but it didn't align with anything, which created a major eyesore (illustration p. 82).

I now ask electricians to locate smoke detectors on walls centered above doorways in each room that is required to have a detector. The ideal location is 6 in. to 8 in. from the ceiling, but check local codes for the maximum distance allowed in your area. The ceiling stays unblemished, and the smoke detector's position has some rhyme and reason. When it isn't possible to wire in a smoke detector above the door, try to locate the detector on the ceiling a few inches out from the sidewall but still centered on the doorway.

If a ceiling has an unusual shape, such as a cathedral or barrel-vaulted ceiling, I prefer to center a smoke detector on the wall directly below the highest point, again keeping the ceiling free of unnecessary clutter (illustration

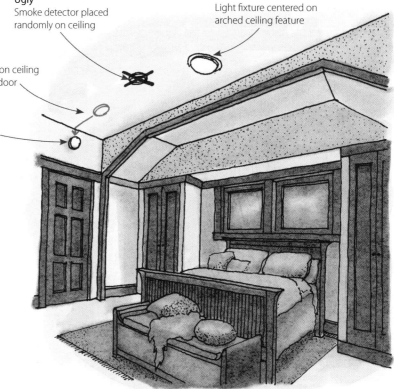

Ugly
Smoke detector placed randomly on ceiling

Light fixture centered on arched ceiling feature

OK
Smoke detector on ceiling centered over a door

Best
Smoke detector on wall centered over a door

Keep ceilings uncluttered. Ceiling light fixtures should be placed symmetrically with features such as an arch. Smoke detectors should be centered on the wall over a doorway or just above on the ceiling.

Ceiling looks better when kept clear of smoke detectors and security devices.

Smoke detector

right). Because there is no standard practice when it comes to smoke detector placement, be sure to go over this request with your contractor and make sure that it gets relayed to the electrician. While yours might not be a typical request, it will make a big difference to the final appearance of each room that's affected.

Security systems

Security systems often have their own smoke and heat detectors connected to an alerting system at the security company's offices. These detectors do not meet local building-code requirements, so they end up duplicating existing detectors, and you can't eliminate the code-required detectors just because you have another system as well. The unfortunate result is that two smoke detectors have to be located a short distance from each other.

In these cases, detector locations should be reviewed with both the electrician and the security installer. I've found that with security-system companies, the person you speak with to arrange for the service is rarely the installer, so make sure that the installer is apprised of your wishes about detector location as well.

Another security-system feature is the motion detector—usually a small rectangular eye—that casts its beam across major traffic paths in the house. In simple houses with unembellished interiors, motion detectors can be almost anywhere and remain inconspicuous. But if the house has special interior finishes, such as wood paneling or elaborate trim work, be certain to review motion-detector locations with both the general contractor and the security-system installer.

On one frustrating occasion, we had installed wide trim boards around a room with intricate moldings and wall finishes. The security-system installer had chosen the most visible corner of the room and had stuck the

Smoke detectors and irregular ceilings. With vaulted or cathedral ceilings, smoke detectors should be centered 6 in. to 8 in. below the highest point of the ceiling.

Moving the detector up a short distance above the wood trim makes it almost invisible.

Keep motion detectors inconspicuous.
Instead of mounting a motion detector on the woodwork where it will stand out, move it to a similarly colored background where it's less visible.

motion detector in the middle of the wide board. To make matters worse, the board was a medium-dark color, and the motion detector was bright white, a sore thumb to beat all sore thumbs. Although the installer wasn't happy about it, we moved the device about 15 in. up the wall to a section painted white, where it all but disappeared (illustration above).

Thermostats and other control devices

Another device that is crucial to home comfort but that is rarely located with any thought to aesthetics is the thermostat. In most houses, thermostats seem to be located on the wall most usable for displaying hanging art, which causes new homeowners major frustration and angst. My solution is to group the thermostat with other miscellaneous control devices, such as the heat-exchanger control panel and the sound-system volume control.

One characteristic of these devices is that they stick out several inches from the wall, attracting even more attention to them. By creating a 2-in.- to 3-in.-deep recess in a stud wall (illustration facing page), they become much less obtrusive. The recess also encourages installers to keep their particular control devices relatively close to the others, which doesn't ordinarily happen.

When locating this recess, I meet with the heating and HVAC subcontractor to decide which locations work most effectively. The thermostat still needs to be in a fairly central location with no direct sunlight, one away from other heat-generating devices. But it doesn't have to be in the center of the most focal wall surface in the house, preventing it from being used to hang artwork. If other control devices are located here as well, consider which location allows most convenient access for each control. If you have an architect involved, it's best to explain your goals and have that person work with the general contractor to arrive at the best solution. Good design can provide room for all the various functions that a wall surface is put to, and nothing need be precluded.

These ideas may seem alien to the residential-construction process. But in working with clients who want houses that are carefully, thoughtfully designed, these issues become important and require thorough consideration. The most important thing I've realized is that these devices are the calling cards of the installers. They want their work to be seen and appreciated. The trick is to convince them that their work will be appreciated more if the devices are placed discreetly rather than prominently.

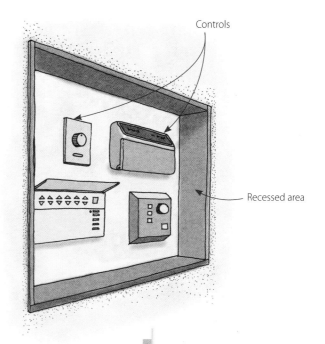

Controls

Recessed area

Recessed area houses all the controls in one place. Keeping all controls, such as thermostat and sound-system control, in one place makes good organizational sense, and recessing the area makes the controls less visible.

If the house has special interior finishes, be certain to review motion-detector locations with both the general contractor and the security-system installer.

FOUR

Making It
Personal

There are few things more valuable in transforming house into home than making the place you live reflect your personality, passions, and interests. Unfortunately, because we've been made to think that adding personality to our houses will lead to some terrible resale faux pas, many homeowners are reluctant to imprint their houses with things they love.

While there are things you can do from a design standpoint that will make a house less attractive to future buyers, these are the exception rather than the rule. I had one client, for example, who wanted a large house but with only one bedroom. That is decidedly *not* a good move for resale. But adding a beautiful tile backsplash in a kitchen or adding a wall of bookshelves in a family room is the kind of thing that has broad appeal while also improving the quality of your life for the time you live in the home. So in this section, we'll look at ways to make your house truly yours by adding features that personalize its character and utility.

One area of the house that often gets short shrift but greatly affects both your own feelings about your house as well as the first impressions of guests is the front entry, both inside and out. Making the process of entering as welcoming as possible builds in value that you'll appreciate every day and, when it's time to sell your house, will bring big dividends as well.

There are also ways to tailor your home to fit the way you live by adding built-ins, such as well-proportioned benches and a table to create a breakfast nook in the corner of a kitchen. When you add features like this, it's important to execute the project well so that it serves your needs but also has value to future residents. These kinds of features, when finely crafted, will make the house seem bigger, while also making it fit you to a tee.

Personalizing your house doesn't have to mean costly design changes, though. In fact, one of the simplest strategies to make your house your own is to use color. When you're on a budget, this is a great way to add personality with the simplest of resources—a can of paint and sweat equity.

In many ways personalizing requires only the willingness to experiment a bit. When you give yourself permission to do so, you'll find that your home has vastly more potential and character than you ever gave it credit for.

Designing a Welcoming Front Porch

Like many people, when I walk around my neighborhood, I'm surprised by the number of houses that lack a welcoming entry. The front door is placed unceremoniously on the street face of the house, amidst windows and shutters, and there's nothing that invites one up to the house other than a path from the street and a set of concrete or brick steps. Unfortunately, most homeowners don't see the front entry as being critically important, so it's usually one of the last areas on the list for remodeling. A well-designed front porch, however, can transform a plain-looking house into a home with real curb appeal. A covered entry also creates a welcoming look from the street and shelters visitors arriving at the front door.

Making a good first impression

Remodeling an entry can be done economically, and it's one of the few remodeling projects that can increase the value of the house by the amount invested almost immediately. Real-estate agents will tell you that first impressions are important: It is easier to sell a house that presents itself well to the street than one that doesn't. Many house showings are sabotaged by the appearance of the exterior. If potential buyers don't like the way the outside of the house looks, it's often impossible to get them inside the door for a closer look. Conversely, a house that welcomes visitors also welcomes prospective buyers, who are far more inclined to like what they find inside the house. Our expectations about the character of a house are shaped largely by what we see from the street.

The best way to illustrate a few simple ways to change a basic entry into a welcoming porch or front stoop is to look at some examples. While those that follow focus on Cape Cods and colonials, the design options are applicable to many house styles. Of course, an architect can also provide options that will best fit your home's style.

Porch options for a Cape

The standard Cape design features second-floor living space housed in the roof, with dormers bringing light into the upper level. As the roof eaves on the front façade are a full story closer to the ground than a two-story house, the face of the house has a cottagelike appearance. This means that whatever roof form is used for a covered stoop or porch will either meet or come very close to the main-house roof. The lean-to roof form and gabled porch are two of the most economical and easy-to-add design options.

The lean-to roof looks like a natural extension of the main roof, and so the small segment of lean-to roof used to shelter the front door area alone seems welcoming. When combined with a full-width porch, which is my favorite option on the Cape Cod, the whole house looks larger. The eye reads the porch area as a part of the floor space of the house because it's nestled beneath an extension of the main roof, which helps to maintain the cottagelike feel of a Cape. A lean-to roof with a pitch that's lower than that on the original house is necessary in order to make it look right.

A gabled porch can also look good on a Cape Cod, provided you can align the peak of the porch gable in some logical way with the dormers above. If the front door is located directly below one of the dormers, as is

Entry options that complement the cottagelike character of a Cape Cod. A redesigned entry should consider both form and function. The space should be useful to the homeowner and inviting to visitors.

A carefully placed gabled entry preserves a Cape's character. The roof ridge is best centered on a dormer, not on the front door.

A lean-to works well on a Cape because it blends into the main roof.

A full front porch is the most welcoming and useful entry on a Cape. It also makes the house seem much larger.

A gabled entry is most attractive on a colonial. An arched ceiling creates a welcoming flow into the house.

A flat ceiling underneath the gable works, as well as an arched ceiling, and it's easy and inexpensive to build.

A lean-to provides shelter but is less inviting on the two-story wall of a colonial than on a Cape.

Options for a welcoming colonial entryway. Many colonials have no shelter over the front door. Although this look is classic, it's not welcoming to visitors or homeowners.

frequently the case, then it's easy to center the porch roof ridge on the dormer above. If the door does not align with a dormer, though, it's best either to center the porch roof ridge between dormers or to center it on one of the dormers. The front door won't be aligned with the center of the covered area below, but this is generally less objectionable than having the roof forms at odds with one another, which is more noticeable from the street.

A welcoming porch for a colonial

Many colonials have no sense of shelter over the front door. Although this presents a classic look, it's not a particularly welcoming face for either visitor or homeowner. There are a variety of ways to provide this sense of shelter, but some are more aesthetically pleasing than others; as with a Cape, both a gabled porch and lean-to roof can be added and still preserve the character of the colonial form. If you are planning only a small covered area at the top of the steps in front of the doorway, adding a gabled roof over the stoop looks significantly more appealing than a lean-to. The sloped roof of a small lean-to almost seems to push away visitors instead of welcoming them in. But a gabled roof can have a curved or barrel-vaulted ceiling, which seems to graciously draw visitors in from the street.

A gabled entry stoop with a flat ceiling can work as well, but it's not as engaging: The horizontal line at the base of the gable form suggests a barrier to movement, while the curved ceiling, like a segment of tubing, moves your eye in the direction of flow. These may seem like subtle distinctions, but it is amazing how sensitive we are to these visual cues.

Another option for a colonial is to add a front porch across the entire front face of the house, though it looks best if the roof edge sits back a foot or two from the side face of the house at either end. Unlike the short section of lean-to, the length of the porch form eliminates the sense of being pushed away. With this approach, it's important to use a low pitch for the lean-to roof—perhaps 3:12 or 4:12 at most. The mistake is often made of matching the porch roof pitch to that of the main-house roof, which is typically quite steep on the traditional colonial. Although this may seem logical, the result is a roof that looks too sloped. It is best to make a front porch like this at least 8 ft. deep, making the

area usable for sitting purposes, but even a 6-ft.-deep porch will work. From the street, you still have the impression of a graciously proportioned, covered entry porch.

There are many elements that make each style of porch look good and appear in proportion to the surrounding façade. If you're planning an entry porch remodel, first become a keen observer of the entryways in your neighborhood. Take a camera with you when you walk or drive around the area, and pay attention to what works and what doesn't. And consider hiring a design professional to help ensure that your investment will make your house more appealing from the street and more welcoming to you and your guests. Changing or adding a porch may seem like a small remodeling, but it has the potential for big impact if you do it well.

Full-length colonial porch. A larger porch adds an inviting entry and usable outdoor space to a colonial.

The Importance of a Front Entry

Homes that don't have a front entry, or foyer, tend to make a bad first impression. If you've ever been to a house that shoves you unceremoniously into the main living space as soon as you step through the front door, you'll know what I mean. When people are outside and "in public," they wear not only clothing appropriate to the outdoors but also their public persona. Once inside a house, whether it's their own or a friend's, a significant shift of persona typically takes place, making them more at ease and less guarded.

A front entry, or receiving place, is crucial to a sense of welcome, inviting the visitor to step in from the outside world. But how can you make such a space if none exists or if the one you have is cramped or dark? There are many solutions, but to implement them successfully, you should understand the characteristics of what I call psychological breathing space—the tailoring of the space to make people feel that they are in a well-defined place that's separate from the adjacent room or rooms.

A front entry, or receiving place, is crucial to a sense of welcome, inviting the visitor to step in from the outside world.

Carving entry space from the living area

The best way to illustrate what works is to look at a couple of common examples. Let's start with a standard ranch house. Many of these houses that were built just after World War II were intended to provide good shelter but few frills. Unfortunately, a front entry was considered a frill, and so it was

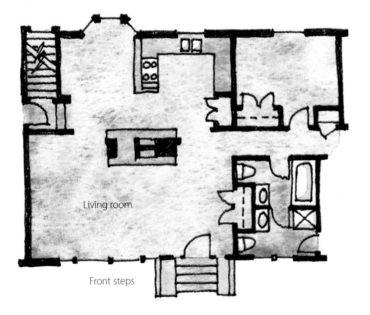

Front door opens
directly into the liv-
ing room.
Without any separa-
tion between the
entry and the living
room, visitors have
no place to make the
transition—physically
and psychologically—
from outside to inside.

Living room

Front steps

omitted. In lots of houses, you step from the front stoop directly into the main living area, where the major family activities happen. A guest walks through the door and into the middle of people watching TV, kids playing, and dogs barking. A greeting like this can make a visitor want to turn around and leave. Even the homeowner surely wants a more graceful welcome.

The first part of the solution is to add a surface to stand on that's not part of the flooring of the rest of the room. But it's not enough to change just the floor material. Although this provides a small amount of differentiation from the rest of the room, it

doesn't create a separate place. For this we need a three-dimensional boundary, a sense of shelter around the new patch of floor.

Often a homeowner adds a small half-wall to divide the receiving place from the rest of the room, but even this is not enough. You still feel as though you have stepped into the living room. In fact, it is often worse because now the room feels chopped up and awkward. To give a real sense of shelter, you have to define the new entrance at the ceiling level as well (illustrations p. 94).

A valiant but unsuccessful attempt at a foyer. A small area of tile and a half-wall are not adequate to make a welcoming entrance because separation from the living room is not well defined.

A foyer with a sense of shelter. A ceiling beam and walls mark the entry space as distinct from the living area. A simple bench provides a place to set down bags or remove shoes.

An entry that uses more of the room. This entry extends to include the coat closet and provides shelves in the living room for books and display. While this takes more space from the living area, the clear demarcation of rooms makes both spaces work better.

Carving out space for a foyer from the living area will, of course, result in a smaller living room, but the solution that has the least impact on square footage is not always the most livable solution. The key is to find a design that allows both the entry and the living room to function best. Although the living room is made smaller by creating a new entry, the furniture arrangement often works better, and that makes the room feel more comfortable. Meanwhile, the new receiving place gives guests some psychological breathing space, and it flows naturally into the other circulation space in the house.

Brightening a dark, cramped entry

A dark entryway makes the whole house feel oppressive, so it's important to introduce some natural light into the space. This can be done most simply by replacing the front door with one that includes some glass. If you are concerned about privacy, use art glass or obscuring glass. You can also add a sidelight or a window somewhere in the entryway. Either solution will have a huge impact on the way you feel when you enter the house and will even carry through to other parts of the house.

In many cases, a small, dark front entry will be adjacent to the staircase. All the circulation between the main floor and the upper level moves through this entry space, so family members are constantly passing through a cheerless area. Adding a window at the base of the stairs and some glass to the front door will brighten the entry dramatically.

If the remodeling stopped there, however, the entry still would be cramped. Removing a front hall closet, for example, would make the space bright, open, and welcoming. The closet could be relocated nearby, say, under the stairs, or replaced with an elegant coat rack, and the reclaimed space would allow the entry to feel more comfortably scaled (illustrations p. 96).

The new receiving place gives guests some psychological breathing space, and it flows naturally into the other circulation space in the house.

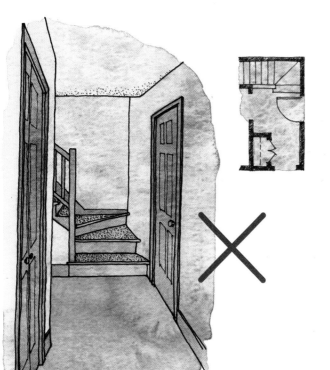

The crucial ingredients of a good front entry include a sense of three-dimensional definition, enough square footage to give you a place to stand and shift from outside persona to inside persona, access to natural light, and a connection to other circulation pathways through the house. When all these characteristics are present, the comings and goings in your home will be more gracious and enjoyable experiences. And you'll find that you like the whole house more, too.

A dark vestibule is not welcoming. This small entrance space has no windows, a closet that takes up much-needed room, and a door that blocks stairway traffic when opened.

Small changes make a big difference. Adding windows in the wall and door, relocating the closet, and reversing the swing of the front door all help to make this a bright, welcoming foyer.

Designing a Breakfast Nook

I've often encouraged my clients to consider a built-in booth, or banquette as they're sometimes called, when accommodating an informal eating area in fairly tight quarters. The downside to a built-in booth is that if it's poorly designed (bottom illustration p. 98), you have to live with its dimensions. Our bodies are particular about what feels comfortable, so it's critical to find out what your household members prefer.

A good way to determine the proper proportions for a booth is to visit restaurants that have booth seating. Bring a tape measure, along with a copy of one of these illustrations, and write down the booth's dimensions and your comments. These notes will help you to tailor the proportions of your own booth.

Begin with the seat

As with a chair, a comfortable bench depends on the shape and size of your body. What feels good to someone who is 6 ft. tall with long limbs will be different for someone who is 5 ft. tall and stocky. I've found a happy medium to be about 20 in. from front to back of the sitting cushion, with a slight tilt to the padded back (illustration p. 99). Too much slope and you will feel too far away from the table surface when you lean back. The height from the floor also varies depending on your body size. Somewhere between 17 in. and 18 in. to the top of the cushion (provided that it's a firm one) usually works for most people, allowing them to sit with their feet on the floor.

It's best to incorporate an overhang between the edge of the seat and the base of the bench, the equivalent of a toe kick on a kitchen cabinet. The overhang allows people

A breakfast nook for informal meals. Built-ins are ideal for squeezing an eating area into a small space. Often designed around a window, they allow everyone to have a view.

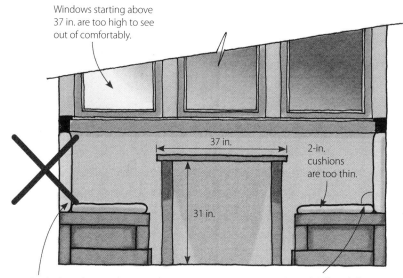

Windows starting above 37 in. are too high to see out of comfortably.

37 in.

2-in. cushions are too thin.

31 in.

Don't place the cushion directly against the wall.

The table is too tall and too wide.

A 90° angle between seat and back is uncomfortable.

A poorly designed booth. A common mistake is to have no overlap of the seat and table. Without this overlap, you have to balance on the edge of the seat to be close enough to your plate. The seat bottom should extend beyond the bench support to create a kick space for your feet. The table should be supported by a pedestal since side legs make it nearly impossible to enter or exit or enter the booth.

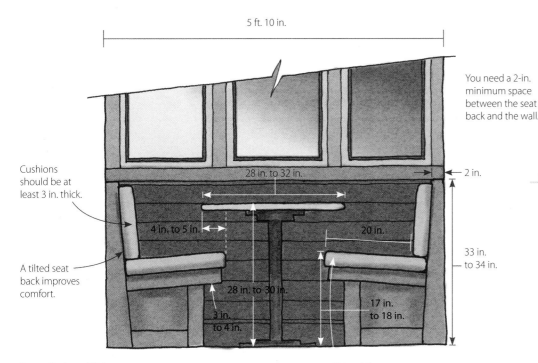

5 ft. 10 in.

You need a 2-in. minimum space between the seat back and the wall.

Cushions should be at least 3 in. thick.

28 in. to 32 in.

2 in.

A tilted seat back improves comfort.

4 in. to 5 in.

20 in.

33 in. to 34 in.

28 in. to 30 in.

3 in. to 4 in.

17 in. to 18 in.

Several inches of kick space let you position your feet comfortably and make it easier to slide into the booth.

Extend the cushion beyond the support.

Built-in booth basics. Begin with the range of dimensions shown here for someone of average height and medium build. The width of the booth needs to be only 5 ft. 10 in. If you have extra room, increase the width of the ledge behind the seat back rather than the table width; it will make the booth seem more spacious and comfortable.

to place at least one of their feet a little behind their knee without banging a heel into the bench support.

Back heights can vary

A wide range of back-support heights works for most people. The lowest level I've used had the top of the cushion 27 in. off the floor. With this minimum, it's important to have a bit of a sill or ledge above the cushion so that when you lean back, your head doesn't hit the wall. Even if it's just a couple of inches wide, this sill gives the booth a more spacious feeling. Make certain,

however, that the sill does not protrude out beyond the vertical seat back, as it will cut into the sitter's back.

One of the reasons for selecting a low back is that it allows adjacent windows to be located closer to the height of the table itself, which in turn connects you much more strongly to the outside, one of the most delightful aspects of a booth.

If you'd rather have a taller, more comfortable back support, increase the top of the cushion to 33 in. to 34 in., which makes it more like a couch and encourages hanging around the table after a meal.

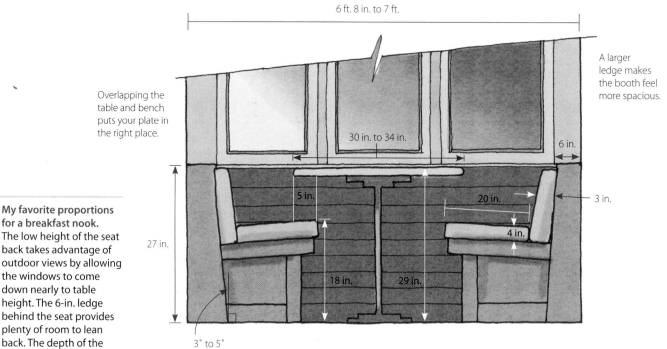

6 ft. 8 in. to 7 ft.

A larger ledge makes the booth feel more spacious.

Overlapping the table and bench puts your plate in the right place.

30 in. to 34 in.

6 in.

5 in.

20 in.

3 in.

4 in.

27 in.

18 in.

29 in.

3° to 5° from vertical

My favorite proportions for a breakfast nook. The low height of the seat back takes advantage of outdoor views by allowing the windows to come down nearly to table height. The 6-in. ledge behind the seat provides plenty of room to lean back. The depth of the seat can vary with the length of your legs, but I've found that 20 in. is a reasonable average.

The table should overhang the bench

This is the feature that is most frequently botched. When you're seated with your back against the cushion, the table edge needs to be close enough so that you can comfortably move food from the table to your mouth without crumbs falling in your lap. When I first started designing booths, I was surprised to discover that I needed an overlap of several inches. Many restaurants align the table edge and bench front so that you have to perch on the edge of the seat to get close enough to your plate. But the perching usually makes one feel quite uncomfortable. I prefer a 4-in. overhang, while others have

told me that 2 in. is plenty for them, so in your measuring exercise this is an important dimension to check.

Create a table with the right proportions

Frequently, booths have a table that is too tall for the benches. As with a dining table, the height that seems to work best for most body types is around 29 in. If you are short, you might want to reduce this height by an inch, and if you are tall, you could raise it by an inch. But if you do so, recognize that your average-shaped friends may find the arrangement a bit awkward.

If your booth is intended primarily for eating and if people will be seated on both sides, I recommend at least a 30-in.-wide table. If you go beyond 36 in., you'll find that the person on the other side of the table feels awfully far away. Just because you have room to make the table wider doesn't necessarily make it the right thing to do. If you've got a few extra inches, add them to the sill width at the top of the seat back. You will give the booth a more spacious feeling without compromising the functionality of the eating area.

And a rather obvious feature of a banquette table is that it should have a center leg rather than corner legs, in order to facilitate ease of coming and going. There is a certain amount of scooting in and out of bench seating with a booth, so making this as unobstructed a process as possible should be a priority.

Cushions enhance comfort

For the seat and back, I recommend using at least 3-in.-thick medium- to firm-density foam for the cushions. A good upholsterer can advise you about the specifics of foam density, fabric choice, and detailing, as well as additional padding and securing options. I've made the mistake of using too thin a cushion for the back support and know unequivocally that 2 in. is just not comfortable.

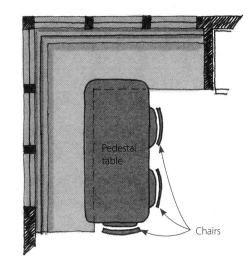

Pedestal table

Chairs

An L-shaped booth has advantages.
An L-shaped booth with a pedestal table lets you adjust the distance between the benches and the table. Chairs on two sides work well for people who have difficulty getting in and out of booths or for parents of young children who have to get up from the table frequently. Unlike a standard booth configuration, the L-shape also allows seating at both ends of the table.

A note about children

Although children's bodies obviously have different proportions than those of the adult users, children are willing and used to contending with less perfect proportioning. So design for the adults, and let the kids kneel if they need to or use a booster chair. Kids usually love booths because there's more of a sense of enclosure as well as proximity to other family members. One further advantage of a banquette—if you have several children at the house, you can accommodate more pint-sized bodies around a banquette than around a regular table.

When a booth is designed to fit, it's a wonderful place to eat and to socialize. But take the time to get the dimensions right. It will make all the difference in your enjoyment of the booth.

101

Make Your House an Expression of Yourself

A house that expresses something about the people who live there is always more engaging than one that's generic. There are so many sources of information these days about how to decorate a dwelling, but it's rarely noted that if a house is to feel like your home it must be filled with those things that have meaning to you. I've been surprised on several occasions when, after spending months working with clients to design a house that fits their lifestyle and tastes, they hire someone they barely know to "accessorize" the place. A few weeks later, the house is filled with stuff that's often as inexplicable to the homeowners as to the visitor. The end result may be beautiful, but because the homeowners haven't participated in the selection of accoutrements and artwork, the house is no more than a stage set for living.

To some, personal expression in home decorating comes naturally. Most of us, though, need help to overcome the fear that we're not doing it right. A couple of years ago, a friend invited me to her home to help her hang artwork. When I arrived, I was stunned. She'd been collecting Navajo rugs for more than 20 years. Each was extraordinary, yet she'd never displayed any of them, never allowed herself the joy of seeing them each day, because she was afraid they might not look right. Don't worry about what anyone else thinks. Your house is for you and your family, not the neighbors. If you aren't sure where to start, here are steps to help you.

Don't worry about what anyone else thinks. Your house is for you and your family, not the neighbors.

Inventory the possessions that have meaning to you

Sit down and list all the meaningful items that have the potential to decorate your home. Don't hold back in this exercise. If you're not sure whether something is appropriate, write it down anyway. Putting it on the list doesn't mean you have to use it, but you may discover options that you'd never have considered otherwise.

For example, years ago during a long walk, I found a large leaf with only the intricate vein patterns intact. I placed this fragile skeleton between the pages of a book and carried it home. It was such a spectacular example of nature's complexity that I decided to frame it, and it has graced my living-room wall ever since. While it's not a conventional work of art, it's exactly the kind of thing that inspires me, recalling the moment of its discovery as well as the magnificence of the natural world. You may have collected similar treasures but because they're outside the normal definition of art, you've hidden them away. Those things are all fair game in making your home a more personal place.

Although it may seem obvious, it's also important to recognize that there are many things we believe we "should" display but don't like. If you don't like the object, whether it's an heirloom, a painting by grandma, or a trinket from a best friend, don't display it.

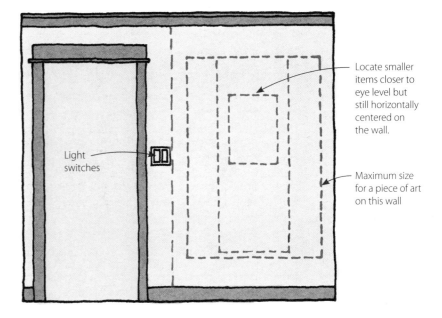

Light switches

Locate smaller items closer to eye level but still horizontally centered on the wall.

Maximum size for a piece of art on this wall

Diagram a wall for better placement. Consider elements such as switches and moldings when centering art.

Identify the display surfaces in your home

Once the list of possibilities has been created, the next step is to identify display areas. Some places already may exist, and some will need to be made. Even if you already have artwork hanging, I suggest listing and diagramming every space and surface available because you may decide to move things around. Measure wall surfaces carefully, and diagram both the width and the height, making note of any light switches, wall outlets, or other items that might restrict the available space. You also may want to indicate the approximate area of the maximum size for a piece on each wall surface. If an object or hanging is too large, it can make the whole space look cramped and awkward (illustration above).

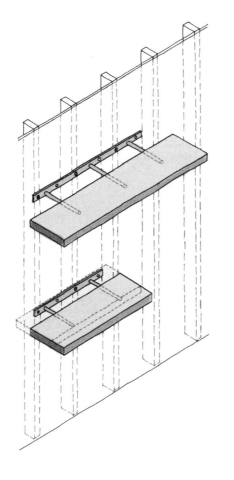

Use wall shelves for display.
A number of simple, inexpensive wall shelves give home-owners the option of adding small display areas without major expense.

If you have a limited amount of wall space in the house, you may want to choose only the smaller pieces on your list. Size might even become a characteristic of the pieces you display, requiring viewers to step up close to each piece, bringing a sense of intimacy. Conversely, if you have many large expanses of wall surface, you may choose a larger object for each to create a pattern of focal points throughout the house.

Many homes have limited shelving space, but this problem is remedied easily. Some excellent wall shelves are available (IKEA®, www.ikea.com; Pottery Barn®, www.potterybarn.com; West Elm®, www.westelm.com) that add display surfaces here and there (illustration left), without having to build or purchase an entire shelving unit. As with wall surfaces, it's important to diagram the dimensions of the space available. Be sure to record the depth of the shelf surface as well as the length.

On occasion, a piece of art or a group of objects demands a special design. Some people have collections that bring them great pleasure, yet they're hidden away because their owners aren't sure how to accommodate them. Those objects can be turned into wonderful everyday exhibits. I once worked with a client who had a collection of small boxes from many countries. He didn't have anything in them but loved their crafting and their amazing variety. We created a wall of shelves to display them and to act as a room divider (illustration facing page). Each box could be appreciated individually, but the entire collection could be enjoyed at a glance. Although many collections may seem idiosyncratic, they make a house unique and delightful.

Room dividers serve a double purpose. A room divider can double as a display area for a collection of objects. The shelves are open on both sides, allowing views from one space to the next and views of all sides of each object.

Rather than deciding what goes where right away, you may want to spend a weekend or two experimenting.

Experiment with what you have

With a record of all the possible places for display in hand, you are ready to experiment. Rather than deciding what goes where right away, you may want to spend a weekend or two experimenting. This process is easiest when two people are available so that one can hold the piece in question while the other stands back to look. If there is more than one decision-maker in the house, take turns to look and evaluate.

Once you've decided on an object for a particular wall, you need to decide on its appropriate location. There are no hard and fast rules here. Look at the object's relationship to other elements on the wall. If you're positioning a long piece like a scroll, for example, you may want to hang it at the same height as the top of the adjacent doorway. If it's a smaller piece, though, you'll want it to be closer to eye level and probably centered in the space available (illustration p. 103). If you find yourselves arguing, give that area a break and come back to it later.

Observe the piece up close, and then stand back and see how it looks from a distance, too. People often are confused by what to do with alignments. It may seem logical to hang something in the center of a wall, but if you always approach a particular wall from

off center (for example, at the top of a stair), you'll want to align the piece with your direction of movement (illustration left).

Identify the visual holes that need to be filled

With the hanging and displaying complete, you'll probably still have some places that need an indefinable something. Rather than rushing out to find that perfect thing, I recommend that you wait and see what shows up over the coming months. If you know the dimensions of the wall and keep your eyes open, it's almost inevitable that just the right thing will show up.

As with almost everything that feels real, decorating a place to express yourself can't be done in an afternoon. And although working with a decorator can be helpful, that person can't do the job without your involvement. A wonderful thing happens when you allow your life's significant moments and acquisitions to color the present. It's not nostalgia but rather the feeling that stems from knowing where things come from, the circumstances behind each object in the house. Taken together, these items capture a taste of your essential nature and inspire your life every day.

When locating art, consider point of view. Another consideration when locating a piece of art is the direction from which you'll see the piece. In this stairway example, the art is best situated in line with the center of the stair run rather than the center of the wall.

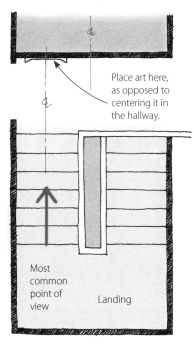

Place art here, as opposed to centering it in the hallway.

Most common point of view

Landing

Use more tha[...]
one color on [...]
The lowest p[...]
be a darker c [...]
a solid base. [...]
ceiling can b[...]
shades of the [...]
complement [...]
trim color sh[...]
wall colors.

Using Color Effectively

The two colors can be shades of the same color or complementary colors. The differentiation of upper and lower parts makes the room seem both larger and more comfortable because our eyes interpret the area above the dividing line as extra space, while the deeper color of the lower part wraps around us like a visual blanket.

Use a strong color in alcoves and wall insets

Another favorite strategy for introducing a significant punch of color in a limited way is to isolate the areas of strong color to places such as wall insets, walls behind bookshelves, the area above fireplaces, and alcoves (illustration right). These are focal points of the room that you want to attract attention to anyway. The color simply reinforces this focus.

When you are designing from scratch, you can add in such spots. By introducing several

of these colored focal points, they c[...] define a theme for the house and m[...] more memorable.

Whatever strategy you use for in[...] color into your own home (or into t[...] you design and build), don't be shy. to color and use it boldly. When do[...] color adds both vitality and delight experience of living there.

Adding some color to a home's interior is something that almost everyone agrees is a good idea. After all, color adds vitality and character. It can significantly alter the ambience of a place, whether inside or out. And it can deeply affect our impressions of a house, depending upon our own color preferences. But when it comes to actually picking the particular colors to be used in a home, most people get cold feet and settle for something safe, like off-white or earth tones. Although there's nothing wrong with either, other colors can add more of your own personality.

Paint is relatively inexpensive and easy to experiment with, but many homeowners

The difference between the same room with and without the colored wall is striking.

still have not ventured beyond basic beige. I believe there are two reasons for this. One is that often couples cannot agree on which colors to use because their personal preferences differ. The other is that there is little guidance to help people figure out *where* to add color.

I can't help much with the first point, other than to suggest experimenting with a variety of colors until something appeals to both parties. But the second—what to paint and what the effects of that paint will be—does have some ground rules. Follow the strategies below.

Color one wall with a strong color for visual weight

If you want to attract attention to a particular side of a room in order to make it dominant and the point of focus for the room, then paint that entire wall surface with a strong color. The difference between the same room with and without the colored wall is striking (illustrations p. 108). It literally feels like a different shape of space because your eye is pulled forcefully toward the colored wall.

A simple design element can have a dynamic effect. The room feels different with a single wall in a bold color. It can draw attention to or away from something. The wall's color should complement colors already present in the rug, the art, or the view.

A friend of mine has a home in which every room has a dominant colored wall, and each color is different. The character of the house is largely defined by these colored walls. They're the most memorable feature of the house, making it feel lively and bold even though its design is very simple.

108

FIVE

Col
wit

A
the h
perso
stron
same
shad
term
shad
notic
even
very
give
colo
one

Div
a d
and

C
line,
line,
6 in.
add
door
band
dark
colo

Practical
Matters

110

When designing a new house or remodeling an old one, there are a number of issues that frequently get overlooked—issues that can dramatically affect the functionality, and thus the livability, of a home. For example, have you ever been in an older home—perhaps your own—that didn't have a powder room on the main level? Although this is a standard feature in newer homes, in days gone by it wasn't a prerequisite. As any mother of young children will tell you, having to rush upstairs to use the bathroom is not without its disasters!

Finding space for a powder room within an already cramped main level can be a challenge, but looking at solutions in a creative way can make this seemingly impossible task feasible. In this section you'll discover how to make the most effective use of the space you have available to really support the way you want to live.

Like powder rooms, laundry rooms, both old and new, are also often poorly laid out. Even when there's not much space available, you can make the room work efficiently if you understand some of the basic functional requirements and how they relate to one another. Just like a kitchen, a laundry requires some careful thought in order to make it work well. A little preplanning can turn a little-loved task into a relative pleasure. When you like the space you are working in, you'll find that your whole attitude to the task will change.

And then there's the issue of appropriately integrating all the sound generators we have in our lives these days, most especially the TV. This requires some careful consideration to avoid having the TV monopolize the household's attention from the first cup of coffee in the morning to lights out at the end of the day. Because its imagery is so addictive and its sound reach so extensive, if we don't give some thought to where the TV and other electronic devices are located, we can find our "free" time eaten away without even knowing it.

Although it may appear that there's neither enough space nor any way to circumvent the problems inherent in a particular device or fixture, with a little creative problem solving, you can tackle and fix even the thorniest of obstacles to functionality and greatly enhance your home's livability in the process.

Where to Put the TV

Television has become increasingly dominant in our lives, bringing with it both assets and liabilities, from instantaneous access to news and entertainment to overuse verging on addiction. Many people are not aware, however, that the design of a house can make watching TV a conscious choice rather than an ever-present activity.

When I'm working with clients, I'll ask them to make two lists about their television-viewing habits. The first list describes the way TV watching happens in their house at present. Where are the televisions located? When are they used? Are they on when no one is around? How does their placement affect other activities in the house?

The second list describes the way they'd like the TV watching to happen. I will usually ask each adult in the household to make a separate list, as there's often a difference of opinion. To arrive at desirable TV-watching patterns, I'll ask them to consider questions like these: What activities are interrupted or made untenable by the presence of the TV? How often is TV watching affected by other activities occurring in the same space? Are there disagreements related to TV watching and TV placement and what are the solutions?

I tell them not to be alarmed if the lists are substantially different. Typically, there is a way to satisfy everyone as the design process proceeds.

When the TV is in the primary socializing spot, and when that spot is open to most of the other living spaces, the TV tends to monopolize everyone's attention.

General placement issues

Now that flat-screen TVs have become the norm, elegant integration of the TV has become significantly easier to accomplish than it was a few years ago. Since the screen is more akin to a picture frame than a massive box, it takes up less volume and can even become a thing of beauty with the addition of some TV screensaver software (check out ScreenDreamsDVD.com). But there's still the challenge of positioning. Because of the similarity of the shape of the screen to a piece of artwork, by default it often gets located above the fireplace if there is one; however, this is higher than ideal and can give viewers a serious neck ache unless the seating is fairly far back from the wall on which the screen is hung.

A better height is obtained by setting a freestanding or wall-hung unit above a low built-in or piece of furniture composed of drawers, cabinetry, or bookshelves. The benefit of this approach is that it can provide much-needed storage for DVDs and video gaming accoutrements.

In working with many families over the past couple of decades, it's clear that there's no one right answer for everyone. Opinions regarding television run the gamut from taking it for granted that it will be on all day, every day, to disdain for its very existence.

Whatever your comfort level with the issue, the most important thing you can do is to develop a strategy for making your TV-watching habits more conscious and deliberate rather than simply allowing the TV to take control of your life.

Although the previous issues and solutions may seem rather obvious, it is amazing how difficult it is to actually implement most of them. It takes a concerted effort on everyone's part and an appreciation for what you are gaining as a result. When the locations of televisions are carefully considered in the design of your home, you can dramatically improve the way you live and at the same time restore household harmony.

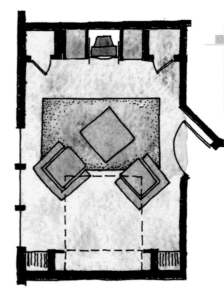

Make a guest room double as a den. With a Murphy bed stored in a wall, a guest room can be transformed into a room for TV watching.

Designing a Kitchen Island

The kitchen is the primary activity area of the house, not only for meal preparation but also for social activity. While preparing meals can be a social event, too many noncooks in the kitchen can make meal preparation difficult. A kitchen island can significantly improve the balance of prep and play by providing an extra work surface for the cook and a sanctioned socializing zone. Kitchen islands allow others to interact with the cook or to join in meal preparation and cleanup (top illustration).

Some kitchens are too small for an island

To design an island that will enhance the kitchen's utility, you have to take certain dimensions into consideration. Some kitchens are simply too small to afford losing floor space; an island would restrict movement severely (bottom illustration facing page). Large kitchens also can have the opposite problem: Often they have large islands, which are hard to move around easily (illustration p. 120).

> *A kitchen island can significantly improve the balance of prep and play by providing an extra work surface for the cook and a sanctioned socializing zone.*

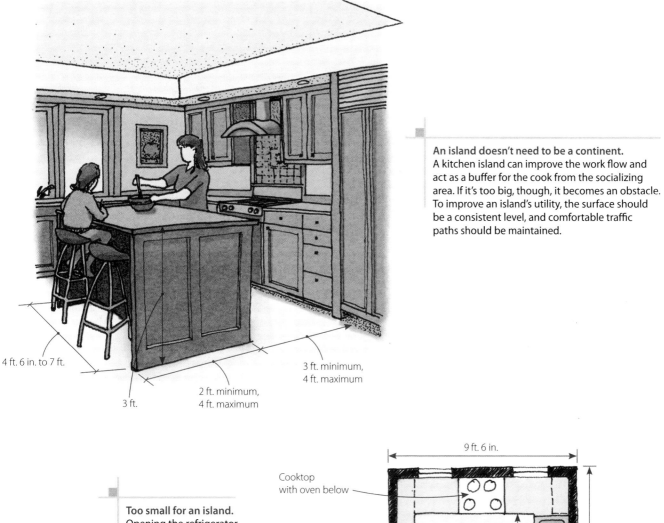

4 ft. 6 in. to 7 ft.

3 ft.

2 ft. minimum,
4 ft. maximum

3 ft. minimum,
4 ft. maximum

An island doesn't need to be a continent.
A kitchen island can improve the work flow and act as a buffer for the cook from the socializing area. If it's too big, though, it becomes an obstacle. To improve an island's utility, the surface should be a consistent level, and comfortable traffic paths should be maintained.

Too small for an island. Opening the refrigerator and dishwasher becomes awkward with the addition of an island, and travel paths become congested. At the very most, a small rolling butcher block could be added.

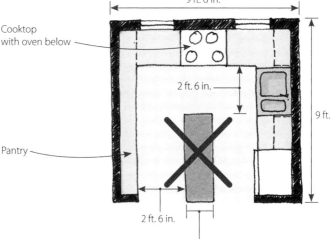

Cooktop with oven below

Pantry

9 ft. 6 in.

9 ft.

2 ft. 6 in.

2 ft. 6 in.

1 ft. 6 in.

Clearances and island dimensions are critical

Like a kitchen, an island can be too big or too small. Islands should be at least 24 in. wide, but 42 in. to 48 in. is ideal. To include room for seating, an island should be at least 30 in. wide (illustration facing page). When it comes to length, the longer the island, the more of an obstacle it can be to bringing things to the other side of the room. Although the best length will depend largely on the size and layout of the kitchen, I find that in kitchens with appliances on both sides

of the room, the best islands are between 54 in. and 84 in. long. If no part of the work area is on the other side of the island, then a longer island will work to serve as the edge of the kitchen. But in these situations, the island isn't really an island but rather a low wall with no upper cabinets, and the kitchen layout is more like a galley with a great view into the adjacent room.

Between the edge of the island and the adjacent countertops, I like a clearance of about 42 in. While 36 in. allows one person to work comfortably, two or more people working together will be bumping into each other constantly. More than 48 in. requires too many steps between island and counter, making the island less useful.

The work triangle

The work triangle provides guidelines, not absolutes. In a nutshell, it states that the three legs of the triangle, linking refrigerator, sink, and cooktop, should be from 13 ft. to 22 ft. long. If it is shorter than this, the cook will have too little work surface between functions, which can make meal preparation awkward. A triangle that is much longer than this will force too many steps between functions, making meal prep and cleanup great as an exercise regimen but frustrating in terms of efficiency and convenience for the task at hand.

Minimum kitchen size for an island. With this layout, there's just enough room for an island but no room for stools. This layout increases utility of food prep but doesn't shelter the work zone as effectively as an island with seating.

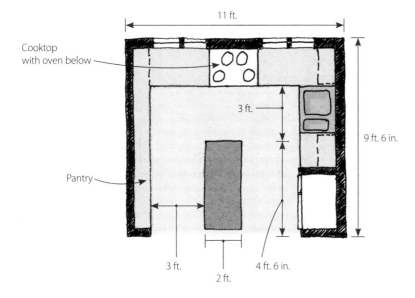

Cooktop with oven below

Pantry

11 ft.

3 ft.

9 ft. 6 in.

3 ft.

2 ft.

4 ft. 6 in.

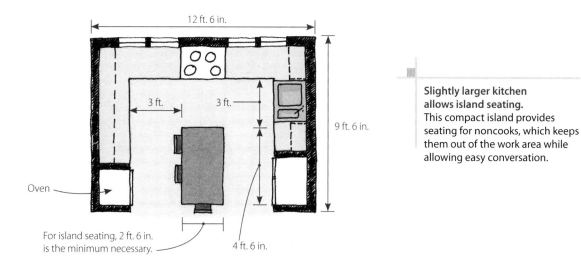

12 ft. 6 in.

3 ft.   3 ft.

9 ft. 6 in.

Oven

For island seating, 2 ft. 6 in.
is the minimum necessary.

4 ft. 6 in.

Slightly larger kitchen allows island seating. This compact island provides seating for noncooks, which keeps them out of the work area while allowing easy conversation.

Standard height is the best height

I stick to the standard 3-ft. height for most countertops, including islands. Because people vary in height, it seems intuitive to tailor the countertop heights. But the reality is that when it comes time to sell the house, a low work surface will be a big deterrent to tall buyers, and a high one will be a serious problem for short buyers. Because cabinetry is such a pricey item, variations from the norm can reduce interested homebuyers dramatically.

An exception to the standard 3-ft. height applies to baking areas, which can be lower than 3 ft. for almost anyone kneading dough. This limited segment of the countertop typically doesn't deter buyers and is often looked upon as a plus. But many baking areas turn into junk and mail depositories because they are difficult to use effectively for other food prep.

I don't recommend raising or lowering the seating area, unless its intended purpose is to separate the kitchen from another space. Although differentiating the eating surface from the work surface seems to make sense, it has many drawbacks. Young children may not be able to climb onto the higher stools, and the separation from the work area means that the seating area's counter can't ever be used as part of the work surface. Keeping both at the same height allows the eating surface to do double duty.

The raised or lowered section also has psychological impact. If the top isn't large enough, you'll feel squished when you sit at the lower segment of the island, and you'll feel small when the person standing on the other side of the island has to talk down to you. The conversation can feel more like a lecture. A higher section, on the other hand, separates one room into two, and anything on the other side no longer feels like part of the work area.

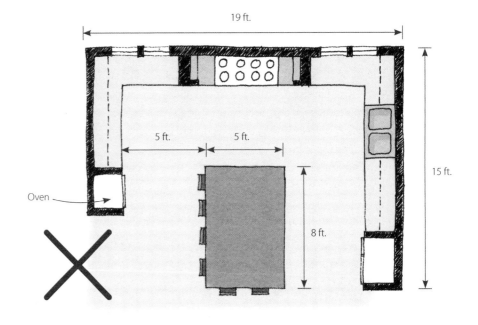

Too big for comfort or utility. This kitchen may look regal in a photo, but it would be difficult to work in because it is too stretched out. The large island is too far from the counter, it's too big to reach across, and it is a chore to walk around.

Island tops can grab attention

Island countertops present the opportunity to use lavish materials on a small scale. Since it is in the middle of the kitchen, the island attracts attention. I often highlight this attention with a contrasting colored material for the island top that complements the surrounding countertops.

Because an island countertop is heavily used, it's wise to choose something durable, scratch resistant, and good looking. Granite, quartz, soapstone, and even high-grade concrete are beautiful for an island and are significantly more affordable than making the whole work surface from this material, though many homeowners are doing just this. I prefer to use the money available more carefully and put the visual splash where it is most noticeable. The most cost-efficient way to use these materials is to have no cutouts, even for a prep sink. Because the materials are so hard, the fewer cuts that must be made, the less expensive the slab will be. Another beautiful and useful surface for an island is butcher block. If you know how to look after it properly, a butcher-block surface can epitomize both beauty and utility.

Having tried several solid-surface options, I'd recommend contacting people who have the surface installed in their house before you decide which to purchase. There are differences in performance and "marability," and although most products promote their ability to be cut on like a chopping block, I know of few people who actually use them this way. We tend to like an unblemished surface, so those that clean up the easiest and that scratch the least tend to be the most favorably received.

Laminate doesn't have to look cheap

If you have a limited budget, there is nothing wrong with laminate. It can look almost as good as a solid-surface countertop, given all the colors available, at a fraction of the cost. On an island, the primary reason that laminate can look cheap is the edge detail. The front and back often are different from the ends, where the material has been unceremoniously sliced through and finished with a piece of flat laminate edging. Ideally, a countertop fabricator will make all four sides look the same by applying a consistently shaped wood or laminate edging all the way around.

One of my favorite tricks to disguise the laminate "look" on the island is to bullnose all four sides but to leave the corners notched out and then to wrap the bullnose edge detail around the corners out of a solid-surface material like Corian®. In fact, this is such a good disguise that most people can't even figure out that the island isn't made entirely of solid-surface material.

A well-designed island can be an enormous asset to a kitchen, providing additional work surface, storage space, and a graceful way to keep noncooks out of the work area. If you have the room, a kitchen island can make food prep more efficient and household harmony attainable.

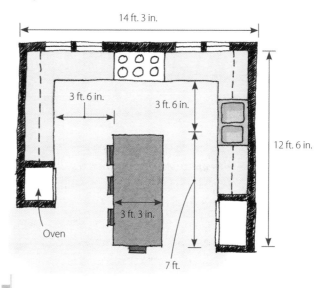

An ideal layout for an island.
This floor plan has plenty of room for two cooks to work together. The island is big enough to share the work surface between food-prep and eating areas.

Squeezing in a Half-Bath

Homeowners often want to add a main-level half-bath to an older home. The problem is that most homes that don't have one are also small, with precious little floor area to spare. With creative thinking, though, there's often a way to tuck in a half-bath.

Steal a little space

While each home is unique, consider these potential spots for a new powder room:

- Take over a closet or pantry. Or move a main-level laundry room to the second floor to make space on the first floor.
- Place a half-bath under a stairway to the second floor (if there is sufficient height to meet code requirements).
- Rearrange the kitchen to free up some floor area to add a bathroom. Ideally it should have a door that opens to somewhere other than the kitchen itself.
- Borrow floor space from an existing porch or sunroom.
- Borrow floor space from a living room or dining room, if the rooms are spacious enough to do so without compromising function.
- Reduce the size of an entry foyer, again, if there is enough space to do so without making the foyer feel cramped.

Architects, designers, and builders are often hard-pressed to come up with solutions if their client is not planning to add space. Under the requirements of the International Residential Code, the smallest room allowed is 30 in. wide, with 15 in. in either direction from the center of the toilet, with at least 21-in. clearance in front of either a toilet or sink to any wall, fixture, or door.

In very tight conditions, I will specify a tiny sink that is about the size of a small drinking fountain but makes a perfectly adequate hand sink. It tucks tidily in the corner, and most building inspectors will allow it to extend into the 21-in. clearance area required by code because it's not directly in front of the toilet

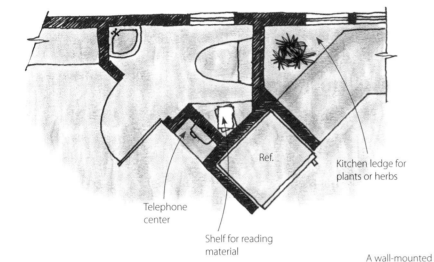

Telephone
center

Shelf for reading
material

Ref.

Kitchen ledge for
plants or herbs

A tiny powder room with flair.
Space for this half-bath was stolen
from the kitchen. The unusual
layout creates interesting nooks in
both the bathroom and the kitchen
and puts the bath close to the
kitchen without opening into it.

A wall-mounted
sink that fits in the
corner saves space
in a tiny bathroom.

bowl. You should always check with your
local building inspector for clearance
specifics because requirements and code
interpretations can vary from place to place.

A pocket door is a great idea for a small
half-bath because the door swing doesn't
have to take up any of the valuable floor
space. If a pocket door is not possible, then
swing the door outward, because an in-
swinging door makes an already cramped
space even more so.

The bare minimum.
A half-bath doesn't
require a lot of space.
Most building codes
call for a minimum
size of about $2^1/_2$ ft.
by $4^1/_2$ ft., with at
least 21-in. clearance
in front of the toilet
and the sink. Local
codes should always
be checked, however.

Think privacy

When space is tight, homeowners are usually not picky about where the half-bath is located. However, there are almost always solutions that not only alleviate privacy concerns but also work well from a functional standpoint.

It is important to give the half-bath both visual and acoustical privacy. So you should try your hardest to avoid having the door open off the kitchen or other primary living space, and it is equally important to insulate the walls.

I recommend a fan to disguise embarrassing noises. An exhaust fan is also required by code in any bathroom that doesn't have an opening window, and sometimes even when there is a window. Fans are not that expensive to purchase or install, and they serve two separate and necessary functions—fresh air and acoustical privacy.

Add value—don't take it away

Tucking the half-bath out of sight will make it more comfortable for you and your guests to use and of much greater value if you ever sell the house. A half-bath on the main level is certainly desirable, but if it is in too public a place, it will actually decrease rather than increase the value of the home.

An architect or designer can help you locate and design your half-bath, even if it is minimal in square footage. Many small residential firms do house calls and will prepare a limited set of plans, giving you a solution that fits your lifestyle, your house plan, and your budget, while simultaneously adding value to your home.

A half-bath on the main level is certainly desirable, but if it is in too public a place, it will actually decrease the value of the home.

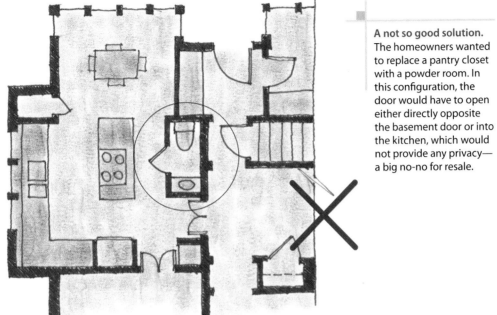

A not so good solution.
The homeowners wanted to replace a pantry closet with a powder room. In this configuration, the door would have to open either directly opposite the basement door or into the kitchen, which would not provide any privacy—a big no-no for resale.

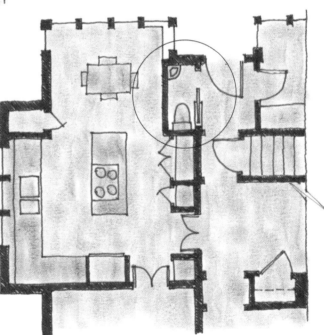

A better solution.
By widening the area next to the back door by 4 in., by bumping into the kitchen eating area slightly, and by using a tiny sink and a pocket door, a half-bath will fit nicely into the back hallway—a much better location.

125

Getting Creative with the Bathtub and Shower

We've all seen those palatial bathrooms with acres of space between sinks, toilet, bathtub, and shower. In more modest homes, however, limited floor space makes a similar arrangement impossible. Is combining the tub and shower a reasonable option to save floor space or has it become passé? Are there occasions when it is appropriate to eliminate a tub altogether? With careful consideration, the combination of the two and—sometimes—elimination of the shower often create the best arrangement for the available space.

My clients tend to prefer a separate tub and shower. Often, they have memories of tiny tubs, too short to lie down in and too narrow to stand in comfortably. Today, though, tubs come in a variety of shapes and sizes. Choosing one that can double as a shower conserves space and, often, money. Be sure to weigh your circumstances and the available options before deciding that a combination tub and shower is not for you.

Considerations for a combination tub and shower

The first feature to look for when you are considering a combination tub and shower is an integral flange on the tub. This flange allows the unit to be located easily in a three-sided alcove, with tile overlapping the flange. Properly installed, the flange ensures that water will not seep between tub and tile (illustration facing page).

The width of the tub is the most critical feature for a shower that is functional and enjoyable.

The right tub makes a perfect shower. A wide tub with a flat bottom and a tile flange on three sides works well as a shower base, eliminating size restrictions common to tub and shower combos.

The width of the tub is the most critical feature for a shower that is functional and enjoyable. Narrow tubs with little elbow room make it difficult to stand and turn around in. Although a standard 30-in. tub may be adequate for a child's bathroom, the addition of a few inches can make an enormous difference for adults.

The tub's bottom should be flat and have a nonskid surface so that standing and moving about are comfortable and safe. A tub with a contoured floor for soaking is not a good choice for use with a shower.

Finally, consider the height of the tub's side. Most tub depths work fine; however, less-agile people should consider how they prefer to enter the tub. Lower sides are better for those who prefer to step in, but with higher sides, you can sit on the edge before throwing your legs over.

There are also "walk-in" tubs available for those with more serious mobility challenges. They have a tightly sealing door on one side that allows the bather to enter before filling the tub with water. While these are ideal for people who are trying to design their home for their long-term needs, they aren't always the most attractive choice, so I would recommend waiting until the need is present before installing one.

Many tubs are eliminated immediately as candidates when the requirements for a comfortable shower are considered. Narrowing choices to the appropriate available models makes the process of choosing a unit easier and more pleasant.

Think creatively to find extra space

Many homeowners make the mistake of assuming that a nice tub must be separate from a shower. In many cases, that's not necessary. If you think creatively and rethink how the current space is being utilized, you might get what you want with relatively minor adjustments. A few inches often make a big difference in small bathrooms.

A couple of years ago, while remodeling a ranch with a fairly tight master bathroom, we were able to give the homeowners an amenity they thought was impossible by simply compromising a few inches. Because the vanity was 48 in. long, it offered us several inches to play with. We replaced it with a 40-in. unit and borrowed the salvaged space for the tub. This additional 8 in. of width allowed us to replace the standard 30-in. combination unit with a much more luxurious soaking tub. The unit remained a tub and shower combo, and the length did not change. We selected a new, deep soaking tub; retiled the tub surround; and replaced the outdated faucets and showerhead, transforming the room into something far more desirable to the homeowners. Although the bathroom still wasn't large, the space compromise gave the homeowners a comfort they thought was unattainable in their home (illustrations left and facing page).

When to eliminate a tub

Many of my clients say they never use the tub in their master bath and keep it only to protect the resale value of their home. I'm a strong believer in building what you want rather than worrying unnecessarily about a future buyer, who may well prefer what you want anyway.

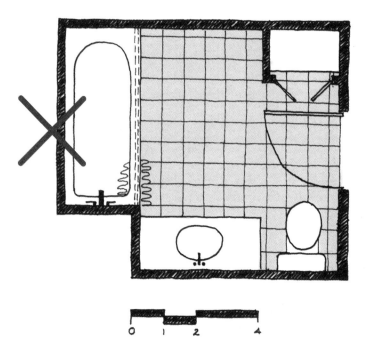

Before remodeling: too close for comfort. A standard tub and shower combination with a rod and curtain provides limited comfort. The tub is too narrow for comfortable showering and too shallow for a relaxing bath.

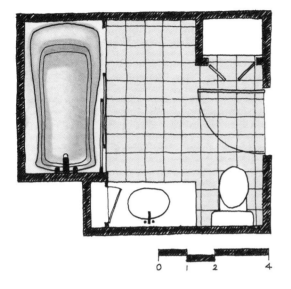

0   1   2   4

After remodeling: a little give and take.
By shrinking the vanity, space was created
for a more desirable soaking tub. The
increased bathing area is accented further
with the installation of sliding-glass doors,
completing the bathroom with an
elegant new look.

If you are building new, and have the space and the budget for it, you can of course include both a shower and a tub, but it's certainly not a "must" today. There seems to be a shift away from the mandatory whirlpool, fueled by the fact that many people rarely if ever use a tub, preferring a spacious shower instead.

If you are remodeling a home with an unused tub in the master bathroom, consider removing it. Provided that a tub is available elsewhere in the house for when there's a young child visiting, I recommend using your valuable space and money to create a well-designed shower in the master bath. The majority of homebuyers prefer a great shower over a mediocre combination.

Another option when space is limited is to place a shower only in the master bathroom and to upgrade the tub in the guest bath. Organizing space in this fashion keeps an enjoyable bathing experience available, without forfeiting quality and character in the home's most frequently used shower. Another benefit of this strategy is that guests have both a shower and a really nice tub at their disposal, making them feel welcome and doted upon, even if they don't actually use it.

The bathroom is one of the most expensive rooms in the house, so consider carefully your own personal patterns and preferences before deciding whether to separate the tub from the shower. Look at borrowing underused space from another room or the existing bath if you need to gain a little more room for what you really want. And don't forget to look at small details that might make your current setup work: Perhaps you can make an infrequently used tub more useful by simply installing a handheld sprayer.

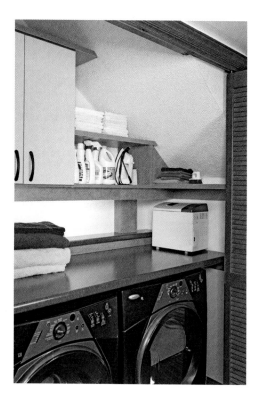

Designing a Laundry Room That Works

When designing houses, many people take utilitarian spaces, such as the laundry area, for granted. Most laundry rooms are filled with machinery, plumbing, and cabinetry, with little thought given to function or aesthetics. If use patterns are considered, though, a laundry area can be made efficient and even pleasant.

A laundry room on the bedroom level, where most laundry is generated, reduces the work of lugging baskets up and down stairs.

Location, location, location

Most laundries are on the house's main level. This placement works well if the person doing the laundry is on the main floor a lot, but other options are worth considering. A laundry room on the bedroom level, where most laundry is generated, reduces the work of lugging baskets up and down stairs. In cold climates where basements are standard, many people prefer the laundry on the lower level, out of sight and earshot. But this location increases basket-lugging, and an unfinished basement frequently makes for an unpleasant laundry room. Still, for nimble people with pleasant basements, this choice can be good.

If the best place is on the main level, a number of options are available. Commonly, the laundry does double duty as a hallway between the house and garage. But few experiences are less welcoming than piles of laundry, the churning and whirring of washer and dryer, and the smell of laundry soap. A better

Elevation

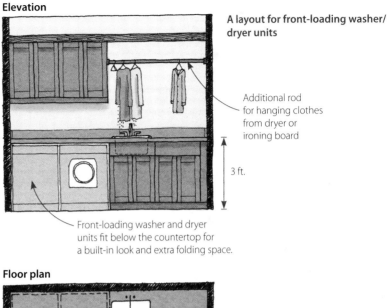

A layout for front-loading washer/ dryer units

Additional rod for hanging clothes from dryer or ironing board

3 ft.

Front-loading washer and dryer units fit below the countertop for a built-in look and extra folding space.

location is a separate room or alcove close to the kitchen and with a sound-deadening door. This arrangement allows participation in kitchen and family-room activities while attending to laundry cycles.

Washer and dryer selection dictates room layout

There are two styles of washer and dryer: side-by-side machines and stacked units. Of the side-by-side units, there are the standard American models (top-loading washer and front-loading dryer) and a newer style, based on the standard European model (front-loading machines). American stacked units come in small and large sizes. The front-loading side-by-side units are great in terms of space because they fit beneath a countertop that can serve as a folding surface (illustrations right). These models also can be stacked.

My favorite choice when space is limited is the full-size stacked units because they take up less floor area and require less bending. You can move items from one machine to the other fluidly. When the dryer load is done, laundry is at shoulder height, easing unloading and folding. One thing to keep in mind is the dryer door swing: It should correspond with the folding surface.

Floor plan

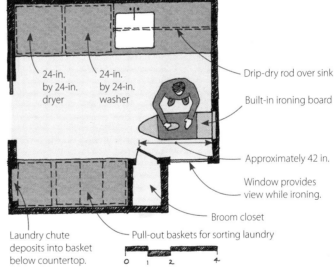

24-in. by 24-in. dryer

24-in. by 24-in. washer

Drip-dry rod over sink

Built-in ironing board

Approximately 42 in.

Window provides view while ironing.

Broom closet

Pull-out baskets for sorting laundry

Laundry chute deposits into basket below countertop.

0   1   2   4

The standard American-style side-by-sides are still many people's favorites (illustrations p. 132). Although they're harder to give a built-in look to, they cost less to purchase and service. Be sure to allow plenty of room for the top-opening washer door to clear upper cabinetry, and if they're placed under

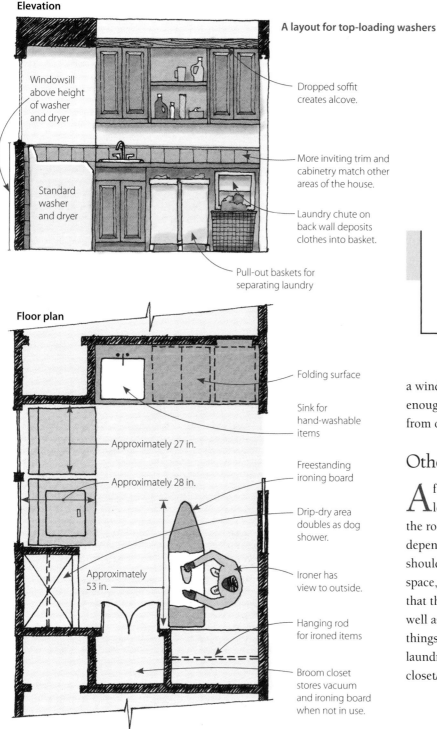

Elevation

A layout for top-loading washers

Windowsill above height of washer and dryer

Dropped soffit creates alcove.

More inviting trim and cabinetry match other areas of the house.

Standard washer and dryer

Laundry chute on back wall deposits clothes into basket.

Pull-out baskets for separating laundry

Floor plan

Folding surface

Sink for hand-washable items

Approximately 27 in.

Approximately 28 in.

Freestanding ironing board

Drip-dry area doubles as dog shower.

Approximately 53 in.

Ironer has view to outside.

Hanging rod for ironed items

Broom closet stores vacuum and ironing board when not in use.

If a laundry room is integrated into the design style and character of the house, it will be a more enjoyable space.

a window, be sure the windowsill is high enough that the tops of the units don't show from outside the house.

Other design considerations

After determining machine type and location, consider what other functions the room will serve. In these decisions, much depends on available space. The laundry area should have a minimum of 3 ft. of counter space, with cabinetry above and below so that there's room to store laundry supplies, as well as a place to put the dirty laundry. Other things to consider are a sink, a hanging rod, a laundry chute, an ironing board, and a broom closet/storage area.

■ **The sink:** Although washers no longer require a sink, many people like having one to hand-wash delicate items.

■ **Hanging-rod/drip-dry area:** A well-designed laundry needs an area for hanging clothes after they come out of the dryer. With a little forethought, this rod also can serve as a drip-dry station. I had a client who wanted a drip-dry rod with a drain and basin on the floor below it. When not in use for laundry, the area doubled as a dog shower. A simpler setup is to locate a rod above the sink.

■ **Ironing board:** A common wish-list item is a built-in fold-down ironing board (bottom illustration p. 131). But at several hundred dollars more than the standard portable, a built-in ironing board isn't always worth it. People often iron clothes somewhere other than the laundry room, such as the family room or the bedroom, so it's important to decide whether the laundry room is really the best location for the ironing board. If not, a mobile unit is the sensible choice.

If clothing will be ironed in the laundry room, allow plenty of room for movement around the ironing board when it is out. Because many avid ironers have a favorite side to stand on while they iron, a built-in model should be placed with this consideration in mind, ideally with a pleasant view.

■ **Broom closet/storage area:** Laundry rooms house soaps and fabric softeners, but often they're repositories of other household items. The vacuum cleaner, brooms, spare toilet paper, and other nonperishables store well here. When determining the amount of storage needed, include these kinds of items if they haven't been accounted for elsewhere.

■ **Laundry chute/sorting area:** Laundry chutes are a real boon in a house with a lower-level laundry. They reduce basket-lugging and simplify sorting. My preference is for the laundry chute to be incorporated into a wall and to empty into a basket under the countertop. This basket can be integrated into the cabinetry and be freestanding or a roll-out type. Ideally, the sorting area will be adjacent to this basket. The sorting area can be composed of roll-out baskets corresponding to the different types of loads. Many interesting products are available for this purpose. It makes sense to select the sorting product, then design the countertop and laundry chute accordingly.

The laundry often ends up being the most boring room in the house. Even though everything works efficiently, this utilitarian room tends to be bland: white laminate cabinets, white countertops, pale linoleum floors. But function is based on more than utilitarian factors. Ambience invites use. If a laundry room is integrated into the design style and character of the house, it will be a more enjoyable place—the final determinant of a room's success.

SIX

Living in the
Real World

In this last section, we'll look at some issues of house design that are related to the broader context of present-day reality. The composition of our homes is changing today, and many homeowners are contending with additional, and often unexpected, members of the household. Blended families can sometimes double the number of people living under one roof, but there are also long-term visitors, returning college kids, and in-laws to contend with. Creating an environment in which there is a reasonable level of privacy for everyone can mean the difference between household harmony and collective misery. Although not all of what arises from the introduction of new residents to an existing household can be solved through the design of the house, a thoughtful layout can go a long way toward keeping the peace.

Another issue that is causing significant challenges in many of our country's older neighborhoods is the teardown phenomenon. As houses age and the land values of inner-ring suburbs increase, new residents want the aesthetic benefits of the existing neighborhood but they also want to make the most of their investment by building a bigger house. The result is often a visual disaster, with the new house grossly outsizing its neighbors and ruining the scale and character of the entire area. Additions to existing homes suffer from the same syndrome. When property values are high, homeowners assume they should maximize the size of a new addition, but in so doing they create an eyesore for all their close neighbors as a result.

There's a better way, and it requires some attention to the context in which the house or addition is being introduced. When you add on or build new in an established neighborhood, the design solution must include not only the homeowner's preferences but also the neighborhood's existing characteristics. I call this being a good neighbor, and it's the way to ensure that our inner-ring suburbs maintain their charm for centuries to come.

By paying attention to your needs as well as those who will be affected by what's happening, you'll create an environment in which everyone can thrive. We are none of us solo flights; we depend on each other. When that interdependence is respected and valued, the natural result is a more harmonious environment—and a better way of life for all concerned.

Making Room for Privacy

Despite the large size of the average American house, many homeowners are almost desperate for a little privacy in their homes once in a while. In a larger home, it's relatively easy to find a quiet spot by rethinking how space is used and adding a door or two. But in a smaller home, the challenge is significantly greater, especially if the household includes a couple of rambunctious kids.

I am always amazed that we haven't fully grasped the idea that humans need privacy as well as togetherness. We aren't always in the mood to be together as a household. Today's homes often have a bedroom for each child, but the master bedroom is a shared space, so there are usually no truly private areas for each adult.

A couple of decades ago, it was not unusual for homes to have a sewing room, which was the domain of the woman of the house. Although most such rooms did contain a sewing machine and worktable, the room could also be used as a simple retreat, a quiet place to go and recharge after a stressful day. The sewing room served an important privacy function that disappeared with the demise of the standard practice of clothes making.

For men, the garage and associated workbench continue to serve a similar function. It's a place away from the social hub of the house, a place that's out of sight and earshot; although garages are rarely glorious abodes, they provide a sanctuary of sorts. It's no wonder that you can find a lot of dads under their cars on a Saturday afternoon: The space is private, small—no room for two—and his domain.

Today's homes often have a bedroom for each child, but the master bedroom is a shared space, so there are usually no truly private areas for each adult.

The recent advent of the in-home office is a step in the right direction, but many homes don't have an extra room that can be devoted to this function. What's really needed is some analysis first of what constitutes privacy for each adult in the household and then some consideration of how best to create a private place or two with these characteristics, given the space available.

The ingredients of a private space

Private spaces allow us to decompress, disconnect from the outside world, contemplate, and recharge our internal "batteries." Depending on your preferences, you'll need some combination of acoustical privacy, visual separation, and physical distance.

For some people, acoustics are key. Common household noise can be disruptive to those who are sound sensitive. They may find music, even of a mellow variety, a major distraction while they're trying to concentrate on something else. These people need acoustical isolation.

For others, visual separation is the most important feature. If another member of the household can see them, they don't feel a sense of privacy, no matter how distant or unheard that other may be.

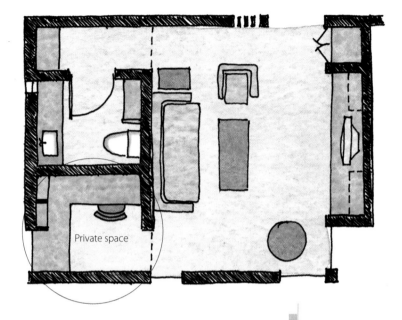

Private space

And finally, there are people who find physical distance from other household members to be the most critical aspect. Privacy for them is about being completely alone, so finding a place that can be both enclosed and at a significant distance from the main social space will be their preference.

Where to find a private space

Many homes have one or two rooms that rarely get used but that don't occur to us as options because they have some other "official" function. Carving out space in a seldom-used formal living room or guest bedroom, for example, can be a great solution. You may want to consider changing the furniture to make one or both rooms do double duty, providing a comfortable private

A small nook tucked out of sight. Away from the main circulation of the room but still close to the action, this space was carved out of a once-larger living room. It has just enough room to spread out work or projects, plus a little bit of shelf storage.

space and perhaps one that can still serve the intended function when it has to. In a smaller house, creating the perfect space isn't always possible, but there's usually a solution that will meet several of your privacy criteria.

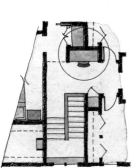

A built-in desk that used to be a closet. Privacy in a hallway is not an oxymoron. This circulation space is not used much during the day, so it is a good place for a work area and a great way to get the most from the square footage in your home.

Create a cozy alcove

If you value visual separation but aren't concerned about hearing the other activities going on in the house, you may be able to create an alcove that's hidden from view but is right off the main living area (illustration p. 137). If it's also important not to be bothered when using this space, you may want to include visual cues, such as a drape or folding screen that, when drawn across the entryway to the alcove, indicates that you want privacy. This option rarely works with small children because they know you are there and can't resist the impulse to visit, but it is usually a successful strategy for older kids and adults.

Even a window seat or sitting alcove can be converted into a private space if a drape is added to one or both sides. When open, the space seems part of the room, but when closed off, it is a cozy and visually secluded retreat.

Transform a staircase landing

Another option for visual separation can be an upstairs landing. In many homes, these spaces are seldom used during the day, when family members congregate on the main living level. So if it's large enough, this area can provide an adequate spot for a small desk or hobby area (illustrations left).

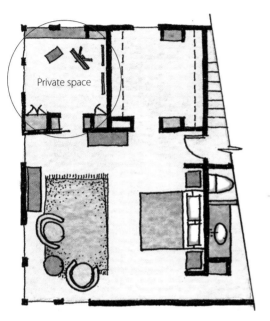

Private space

With a little creativity, you can usually find an appropriate spot for privacy without having to remodel or build a new house.

Private studio space in a master bedroom. An enclosed alcove or a redesigned walk-in closet can make the master bedroom a truly private retreat. This space provides visual and acoustical privacy as well as separation from the rest of the activities in the house.

Carve out space in the bedroom

For those who want significant physical distance from the rest of the household, a basement or attic provides the best alternative. Since for most people, the size of the space is not critical, it may be possible to carve out a corner of a room to serve as a private place. Although the room is ostensibly shared territory, by adding a folding screen across a corner, building a closable alcove, or even adding a loft if ceiling height allows, the room can serve as both a private realm for one and shared realm for two (illustration above).

If the master bedroom is off limits to other family members, this allows for private space as well. With the door closed, children as well as adults understand that privacy is desired.

I have helped a few clients create really private spaces attached to or above a garage or separate structure, which is a perfect solution for someone who desires some distance from activities and noise in the house. Although this is typically a more expensive solution, it can be a dream come true for an introvert.

With a little creativity, you can usually find an appropriate spot for privacy without having to remodel or build a new house. Private space is often right under your nose, and when you start to take advantage of it, it can make an enormous difference to your sense of well-being.

Living with Extended Family

One of the realities of designing a house for our family's future is that we have no idea what life has in store. Due to unforeseen circumstances, we sometimes end up sharing our house with family members we thought were independent from us. Aging parents may need assistance and company, or grown children may return to the "empty nest" for a while. Either alternative presents the household with some critical challenges, both physically and emotionally. When a family member of another generation moves in, it's important to identify what you, as primary homeowners, really want. They are your guests, and you have every right to define how you want them to engage in the life of your existing household.

Get expectations clear up front

Whatever your particular situation, there are issues that need to be addressed for everyone to remain sane. It is always best to talk up front about expectations and to let your new guest know that there will be a family meeting to review how things are going after a specified length of time—perhaps a couple of weeks or a month—where you'll be able to discuss what is and isn't working. If at that point you decide to make some changes to the space he or she now occupies, or even that you will need to add space for your long-term guest, you can draw up a list of design modifications that will help promote household harmony. Good design and clear communication become key ingredients in making such a situation work for all involved.

There's not a single right way for every situation, but here are a couple of examples to help illustrate the problems and potentials of blended households.

One home within another.
A real front door sends a clear signal that this home inside a house is a separate place. Doormat, doorbell, and exterior light fixture add to this impression. The door is adjacent to the back entrance, and both doors open into a shared mudroom (floor plan p. 142).

Grandma comes to stay— for the long haul

A typical situation involves one of an adult couple's parents coming to live with them. Because women tend to live longer than men, that parent is often a mother. Much as we may love those who brought us into the world, we've all experienced the challenges of visiting with a parent after we've left home. Imagine extending that experience indefinitely.

When grandma becomes a permanent member of the household, it's important to talk about the ground rules for interaction and to give her enough private space that she feels she has a home of her own, even though her home is, in fact, part of the main house.

Two friends of mine, Bob and Ellen, recently designed an addition to help integrate Ellen's mother, Maggie, into their lives. For a few months prior to the renovation, Maggie had been living with the couple and their three small children. It had become clear that just giving Maggie her own bedroom and bathroom wasn't going to work. Although Maggie is a quiet and charming woman, her penchant for cleaning was driving Bob and Ellen to distraction. They wanted to be able to relax in the evenings, but they couldn't settle down when Maggie was cleaning. For all parties to feel at home, Maggie needed privacy and a place she could keep the way she liked.

A local architect designed a 20-ft. by 24-ft. addition for them, and, though not large, it gave Maggie her own ground-level entrance off a small private garden space with a single door from her space into the main house (illustrations above and p. 142).

Although she was literally right next door, the entire addition was designed to create a sense of separation and privacy. Even the door connecting the house with Maggie's apartment looks like a front door—a clear visual signal that this is a different place with a different homeowner.

Of course, the addition wasn't the entire solution. Bob and Ellen still held a number of family discussions to help clarify roles and expectations, including a surprisingly dif-

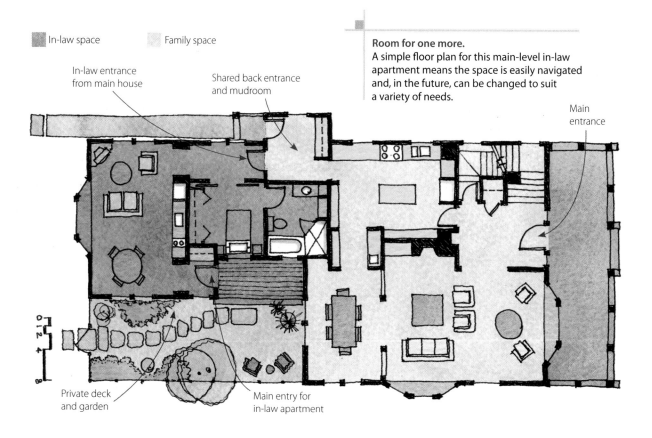

In-law space   Family space

In-law entrance from main house

Shared back entrance and mudroom

Room for one more.
A simple floor plan for this main-level in-law apartment means the space is easily navigated and, in the future, can be changed to suit a variety of needs.

Main entrance

0 1 2 4 8

Private deck and garden

Main entry for in-law apartment

ficult conversation about cleaning behavior, a pattern that proved hard, but not impossible, for Maggie to break.

With the new configuration of space, the family lives comfortably together, without constantly being together. The grandchildren love to "visit" grandma at her place, and she enjoys eating with the family several times a week. The solution was part spatial and part psychological, which is usually the way it goes with multigenerational design.

Twenty-something returns

We usually assume that after high school or college, young adults will be on their own. But that's not always the case. The cost of living continues to increase, there's a more relaxed approach to college education (when to go and how long to stay), and marriage is being put off until later than it used to be. So grown children often see an extended visit home to mom and dad as an excellent financial solution to their cash-flow problems.

A few months can turn into years if you're not clear about expectations. Sometimes parents exacerbate the situation by making it so comfortable that the young adult has no desire to leave. If that's your situation, I recommend that from the beginning you encourage your adult child to think of coming home as an extended visit of a specific duration with a clearly defined end date, and that you charge something reasonable for this benefit.

The spatial challenge can be more confusing. You want your kids to feel welcome, but you also need your own space. Your children will, in all likelihood, see the social space as their space, too, especially if this is the house they grew up in. It was always shared family space before, so why shouldn't it be now? Clear communication is a must if you want to establish different behavior patterns from those that existed a decade earlier.

If your house has a basement or attic suitable for socializing, you might encourage your adult child to make this his primary living space for the time he is visiting (illustration right), unless you want him with you all the time when he's home. Keep in mind that if you make his space too pleasant an environment, with no pressure to move on, he may stay much longer than you anticipate.

There's a peculiar dynamic between most parents and children, however old the child. Things are programmed into us during the first decade of our lives, and thereafter they're hard to shake, no matter how enlightened or mature we may be. There's no magic bullet, and no right way for every situation, but if you keep these simple guidelines in mind, you'll be able to weather the multigenerational household challenge with relative grace.

Adequate but not too comfortable. A walkout basement with few amenities will provide the comforts of home without the temptation to stay long. A small refrigerator, sink, and two-burner stove, along with a fold-away Murphy bed, indicate that the visit is temporary.

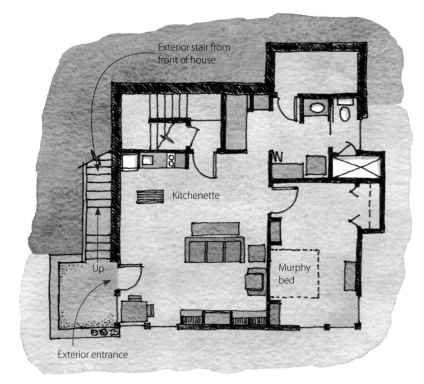

Exterior stair from front of house

Kitchenette

Up

Murphy bed

Exterior entrance

Good Additions Make Good Neighbors

As you walk around your neighborhood, you've probably noticed additions to houses that previously fit in with their neighbors but now are eyesores. Many people don't realize they need the help of an architect or a designer for a successful addition. When they go it alone, the result is often an ugly addition that decreases the resale value of a home (usually by more than they would have paid for professional help) and detracts from the character of the neighborhood.

The most common mistake when adding on is to think about just the floor plan. An addition is three-dimensional, so it should be designed to fit with the existing roof forms, the shape of the house, and the neighborhood. When designing an addition, my goal is to make it seamless, so that someone looking at the house can't tell which part is addition and which part is original.

When designing an addition, my goal is to make it seamless so that someone looking at the house can't tell which part is addition and which part is original.

Begin with the roof

The best way to start planning your addition is to make an accurate drawing or model of the existing roof and walls. For an addition to look good, it has to extend effortlessly from the existing roof.

When adding out, you will want to use roof types that already appear on the house. For example, if the house has a gable roof, then you'll probably want to use a gabled addition (illustrations facing page). Unless the addition is an exact continuation of the

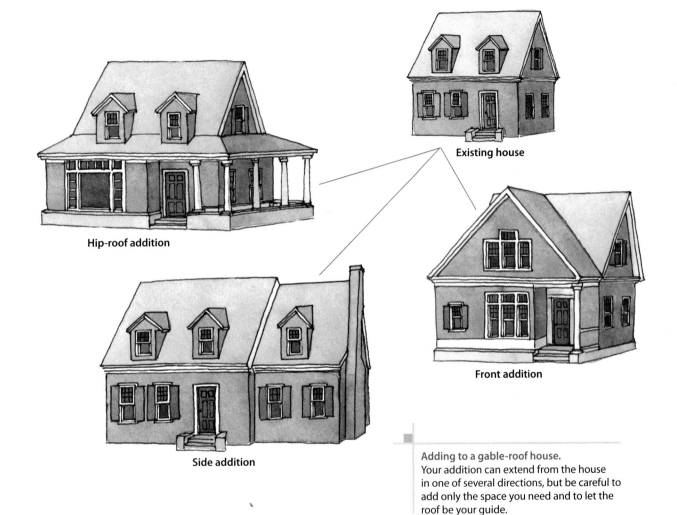

Hip-roof addition

Existing house

Side addition

Front addition

Adding to a gable-roof house.
Your addition can extend from the house in one of several directions, but be careful to add only the space you need and to let the roof be your guide.

main roof, make sure that the roof over the addition is smaller and lower than the one sheltering the main part of the house. This way, you'll avoid overwhelming the original structure both in height and roof size.

A lean-to roof, also known as a shed roof, is a good alternative if you are planning a small addition. It usually looks best with a lower roof slope than that of the primary structure. There are all sorts of other roof shapes, of course, from flat to hipped to turreted, but, in general, if you can mimic the shape of the roof that already exists, the addition will look best.

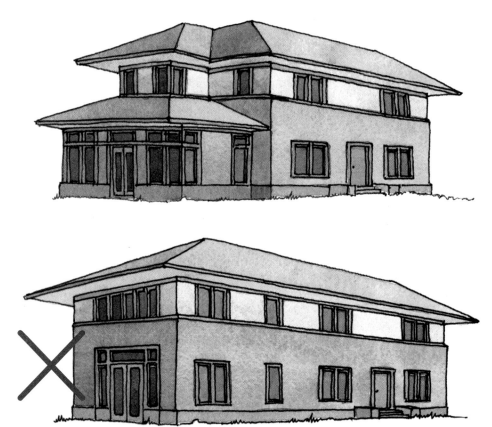

Avoid the monolithic look. Additions that are narrower than the existing house add some character. An addition that is the same size as the original structure will make the house look massive.

Add some personality

Adding on provides an opportunity to give your house more character. An excellent way to do this is to make the width and height of the addition a bit narrower and shorter than the original structure while using the same finish details used on the existing house. An addition that's the same width and height as the original house may be seamless, but it doesn't add much personality (illustrations above).

Assess your space needs

People assume that they'll get the most bang for their buck by making the addition as big as possible, but the results are often disappointing. Outside, the addition overwhelms the house and makes it look disproportionate, while inside, the spaces that are now in the center of the house are dark and unwelcoming. It's better to add on just enough space and also make sure that the existing spaces are well used in the new layout.

Keep scale and detail in sync

For a truly seamless addition, stay with the characteristics of the existing house. You may want to refine these a little, perhaps by adding more windows than in other parts of the house or by using wider trim around the windows. The key is to make the modifications logical extensions of what's there rather than dramatic deviations. An architect or talented craftsman can help you assess what makes sense.

It's important when you add on to notice the basic "rules" of your existing house. For example, if you used very different windows (larger or another style) or placed them differently on the façade of the house, the addition could end up looking like part of a different house.

Think of the neighbors

Finally, keep in mind your neighbors' views of your house when the addition is completed. One of the keys to being a good neighbor when you add on is to recognize that the addition will change not only your life but also those of close neighbors. Your new addition will likely be visible from a number of places within your neighbors' homes, which is unavoidable in most cases, but how the visible faces of your addition are designed can make a big impact on how your neighbors feel about you from this point

For a truly seamless addition, stay with the characteristics of the existing house. The key is to make the modifications logical extensions of what's there rather than dramatic deviations.

forward. Just because you don't want to look into a neighbor's backyard, for example, doesn't mean you have to make the wall they see look like a fortress. Put yourself in their shoes, and design that face of the house to be attractive.

I encourage you to share drawings and models of your house plans with your neighbors. Keeping them informed can relieve their anxiety and make them feel more appreciative of the results. Although you can't always please everyone, a little consideration for the new views that your neighbors will be seeing can go a long way toward building and maintaining a sense of community.

Changing
the Face
of Teardowns

A few years ago, shortly after the world discovered blogging, I was surprised to see a huge spike in the number of visitors to the Not So Big House website. Spikes weren't unusual, but they typically happened as a result of one of my radio or TV appearances. On this day there had been no such appearance. It took me a while to piece together the story of what happened, and it relates to the phenomenon that has come to be known as the "teardown."

On this particular day, a well-known blogger had written about his neighborhood's teardown troubles. He described how he had watched in dismay as house after house on his street had been torn down, only to be replaced by grossly oversized McMansions. The existing neighborhood had been composed of little cottages, and the arrival of the oversized, and in many cases downright ugly, newcomers was creating a great deal of distress throughout the neighborhood. When the fourth such metamorphosis was well underway, he decided to take matters into his own hands. He went out and bought a dozen copies of *The Not So Big House* and placed them on the doorsteps of all those neighbors who had not yet sold their existing cottages, imploring them to read the book and make sure not to sell to anyone who was not favorably inclined toward the Not So Big message.

Historic neighborhoods have been ravaged by an epidemic of teardowns, with many of the charming bungalows being replaced by houses several times larger than their originals.

The arrival of the oversized. Often when a small existing home is torn down, the new owner will attempt to maximize the footprint of the house. When this is done without any design sensitivity, the results can be truly monstrous.

His blog post spread like wildfire as residents of neighborhoods just like the one in which he lived recognized their plight in his words and appreciated his proactive strategy for protecting himself and his neighbors from more of the same.

A national problem

According to The National Association of Home Builders (NAHB), more than 75,000 houses are demolished each year and replaced with larger houses, and the phenomenon has affected more than 300 communities in 33 states. Dallas experienced the demolishing of more than 1,000 older homes, with their replacements ranging in size from 6,000 sq. ft. to 10,000 sq. ft. More than a dozen of Denver's historic neighborhoods have also been ravaged by an epidemic of teardowns, with many of the charming bungalows from the early part of the last century being replaced by houses several times larger than their originals.

One of the main problems, I believe, is that the people who buy a house for teardown purposes often don't recognize that the reason they love the neighborhood has to do with the scale and character of the existing structures. Nor do they realize that the plans they look at in home-plan magazines and on websites are, for the most part, designed for much larger lots in newer suburbs.

The teardown craze may have seemed like an inevitable shift as property values increased over the last few decades and small homes were no longer serving the needs of incoming residents. But there is a better way

Scale and size matter. The most typical teardown replacement is a McMansion, which might look fine in a neighborhood filled with similarly sized homes but looks ridiculously out of proportion in a community of 1940s bungalows and cottages.

to create a home that works that doesn't include replacing all those small gems with uninspiring behemoths. Over the past decade, I've heard from many people looking for a solution to this problem, and though I don't have the final answer, I do have some suggestions that could help alleviate the problem.

The appropriate scale

Plans that are appropriate in scale and detailing for the proportions of inner-ring suburbs are not easily found, though you can track some down with a little research. I've collected a number of offerings from various sources that can be found on the Not So Big House website (www.notsobighouse. com), under the "Not So Big Plans for Sale" button. Two in particular are very useful for older neighborhoods. One is the link to the TND Collection, a set of 240 plans put together by a group of architects and designers to provide Traditional Neighborhood Developments with house design options for new urban communities as well as many inner-ring suburbs. The other is a link to Neighborhood-Compatible Plans, all of which are very much in the same scale as homes in older neighborhoods, where the teardown phenomenon is most rampant.

Professionals who can help

To get the proportions right, it's really important to find the right team of professionals, from architects to building contractors or remodelers, who understand how to make a home that not only works for the way you live but also stays within the scale and character of the other houses in the neighborhood. This isn't always an easy task.

One tool that can help is the Home Professionals Directory on the Not So Big House website, designed to assist homeowners who want to build in a Not So Big way in finding professionals in their area who have the

To get the proportions right, it's really important to find the right team of professionals who understand how to make a home that stays within the scale and character of the other houses in the neighborhood.

A reflection of the neighborhood. A few years ago I designed a new home for an empty lot in a lovely inner-ring suburb. Although it has more contemporary details than its neighbors, it fits in thanks to its proportion and character. It's the house in the middle.

appropriate skills to help them. Although you can also contact professional organizations such as the American Institute of Architects (AIA), The National Association of the Remodeling Industry (NARI), and NAHB, it is often difficult to sort through the listings to find the right match for your particular job. You still need to interview and thoroughly check out the professionals in the directory on the Not So Big House website just as you would when hiring anyone, but they will already know about building better, not bigger.

A neighborhood comes together

Once you become aware of the teardown phenomenon happening in your neighborhood, it's time to organize a committee or community group that can help educate real estate agents, builders, and homeowners about the options that are available. The National Trust for Historic Preservation recently put together a "Teardowns and McMansions Resource Guide," which you'll find on the Not So Big House website, under the " Teardown Alternatives" button. It allows neighborhood organizations to learn from what other communities have done to stem the tide of teardowns. Filled with useful information, tips, and strategies, it should be the starting point for anyone wanting to help preserve the character of their community.

Being a good neighbor

When a house that reflects its neighbors is introduced into the mix, in my experience, everyone concerned is delighted. This was the case when I designed a house for an inner-ring suburb close to a lake in downtown Minneapolis. As we began the design process, we shared our plans with the neighbors so they would know what was being planned. You could watch people's body language as they initially braced for a fight and then breathed an inward sigh of relief as they looked at the perspective I'd drawn to illustrate the future home.

When the house was under construction, the windows in, and the sheathing and roof in place, one passerby stopped to chat with me as I was making a construction observation visit one day. "When did you start remodeling?" he asked. I knew at that moment that we'd won the battle. Not only was the house accepted as a reasonably scaled member of the community, but it also looked as though it had always been there, at least in the eyes of this local resident.

I call this an example of being a good neighbor. If more teardowns were approached in this respectful way, by being woven into the fabric of existing homes, we would not only preserve the priceless value of these lovely neighborhoods but we'd also be strengthening the community for generations to come. A truly Not So Big sensibility if ever there was one.

"When did you start remodeling?" he asked. I knew at that moment we'd won the battle.

Photo Credits

Section One / By Design

p. 4: photo © Grey Crawford, architect: Peter Twombly, AIA, Estes/Twombly Architects; p. 6: photo © Ken Gutmaker, architects: Gail Wong and John Koppe, Gail L. Wong Architects; p. 11: photo by Susan Gilmore, © Meredith Corp., architect: Sarah Susanka, FAIA, with James R. Larson, MSMP; p. 16: photo © Ken Gutmaker, architect: Peter Twombly, AIA, Estes/Twombly Architects, interior consultant: Kirby Goff, Kirby Goff Interior Architecture & Design; p. 21: photo © Ken Gutmaker, architect: Fiona E. O'Neill; p. 25: photo © Grey Crawford, architect: Abigail Campbell-King, AIA, Campbell-King Associates

Section Two / Room by Room

p. 30: photo © Doug Smith, architect: Eric Odor, SALA Architects; p. 32: photo © Seth Tice Lewis, architect: Sophie Piesse Architect; p. 36: photo © Randy O'Rourke, architect: Sarah Susanka, FAIA; p. 40: photo © Dave Adams, architect: Sage Architecture; p. 45: photo © Seth Tice Lewis, architect: Sophie Piesse; p. 49: photo © Grey Crawford, architect: James Estes

Section Three / Attention to Detail

p. 54: photo © Ben Benschneider, architect: Bernie Baker; p. 56: photo © Stanley Livingston, architect: Michael Klement, AIA, Architectural Resource; p. 60: photo © Grey Crawford, architect: Sarah Susanka, FAIA, with Paul Hannan; p. 66: photo © Randy O'Rourke, architect: Tina Govan; p. 70: photo © Grey Crawford, architect: Mark A. Kawen, AIAA, Kawen Mooney Sawyer Architects & Builders; p. 74: photo by Christian Korab, architects: Sarah Susanka and James R. Larson; p. 81: photo © Randy O'Rourke, architect: Sarah Susanka, FAIA

Section Four / Making It Personal

p. 86: photo © Randy O'Rourke, architect: Sarah Susanka, FAIA; p. 88: photo © Anice Hoachlander, Hoachlander Davis Photography, architect: Moore Architects; p. 92: photo © Ken Gutmaker, architects: Tom Ellison and Leffert Tigelaar, TEA2 Architects; p. 97: photo © Grey Crawford, architect: Sarah Susanka, FAIA; p. 102: photo by Susan Gilmore, © Meredith Corp., architect: Sarah Susanka, FAIA, with James R. Larson, MSMP; p. 107: photo © Ken Gutmaker, architect: Laura Craft Architect

Section Five / Practical Matters

p. 110: photo © Greg Premru, architect: Amory Architects; p. 112: photo by Ben Benschneider, architect: Bernie Baker; p. 116: photo © Paul Burk, architect: Cunningham + Quill Architects; p. 122: photo © Robert Benson, architect: Jamie Wolf, Wolfworks; p. 126: photo © Ken Gutmaker, architect: Jamie Wolf, Wolfworks; p. 130: photo © Randy O'Rourke, architect: Sarah Susanka, FAIA

Section Six / Living in the Real World

p. 134: photo © Robert Benson, architect: Jamie Wolf, Wolfworks; p. 136: photo © Shawn Glen Pierson and Architetc, architects: Richard Wiebolt and Shawn Glen Pierson, Richard Wiebolt & Associates Architects with Architetc; p. 140: photo © Steve Oleson, architect: Nick Deaver Architect; p. 144: photo © Anice Hoachlander, Hoachlander Davis Photography, architect: Moore Architects; p. 148: photo © Steve Oleson, architect: Nick Deaver Architect